AH HA! *The* POWER *of* PURPOSE

AH HA! The Power of Purpose
Family, Faith, and A Life Well-Lived

Steve Bartlett

Published by Game Changer Publishing

Paperback ISBN: 978-1-969372-93-3
Hardcover ISBN: 978-1-969372-94-0
Digital ISBN: 978-1-969372-95-7

www.GameChangerPublishing.com

Testimonials

"Steve Bartlett sets forth a master class on how to make meaningful public policy that benefits all Americans. His work reaffirms the essential principles of integrity, hard work, bipartisanship, and respect."

Ralph Neas
Former Executive Director
Leadership Conference on Civil and Human Rights

"Anyone who thinks the government is incapable of solving problems should read these memoirs of a conservative, pro-business Texas politician. As a congressional committee staffer, I worked with Congressman Steve Bartlett on a number of issues. For a member of Congress who wanted to accomplish more than simply getting reelected, he set very high expectations for results—not just actions—and carried that same approach into his role as mayor of Dallas. That, of course, meant long, hard hours for those who worked for him, but they were rewarding because, more often than not, we achieved the outcomes he demanded. One of those outcomes was the Americans with Disabilities Act. Before I read this book, I felt honored to know Steve. I now feel blessed."

Dan Yager
Former CEO
Labor Policy Association

"All the memories recalled in this compelling book emphasize the importance of faith, family, and the sometimes challenging work of coming together to benefit others. They also highlight the value of community involvement, which, as we are learning, is increasingly endangered by the rise of screen time. Steve Bartlett, as a city council member, mayor, and congressman from Dallas, played a significant role in shaping the city's history. Anyone with an interest in Dallas will not only learn from the moments he describes but will also be impressed by how the city functioned and was led toward becoming one of the most desirable cities in the United States."

Rick Douglas

President

Dallas Regional Chamber of Commerce (1991–1999)

What's inside: selected *AH HA!* Moments

What'd You Do, Read the Damn Bill

...It was a Friday afternoon, and Patricia Morrissey came into my office smiling. "Here is the final bill, ready to go to print. Fifteen hundred pages and eighteen months of my life. I'm ready for a stiff drink and a good night's sleep."

.....And the ADA became law. And that law changed the face of America, profoundly...

Set the Mission in Clear, Unmistakable Terms!

...I deliberately set the mission. "We will reduce the number of violent crimes in all four categories: murder, rape, robbery, and aggravated assault within one year."...

...And we reduced the number of violent crimes in all categories in five months, and every month thereafter...

Getting Started

...The culture of my members was clear: CEO's call the shots, we have to modernize the regulatory system if we are to survive, take responsibility, and act fast...

...Finally, and most importantly, light a fire...

God's Plan

...Do I think God had a plan for my life? Well, yes. Just as I believe he has a plan for your life...

...I try to make my purpose God's purpose.

The genesis of this book came from my Grandchildren.

As the reader will quickly note, I am a lifelong storyteller. My most attentive audience has always been my grandchildren, now aged eight to twenty-one. As in, "Grandpa, tell us a story." At the conclusion of every story I always added a lesson to the story, such as "You can be anything you want to be," "Never Give Up. Never," or "The difference between a B and an A grade is huge, but the A only takes a small amount of extra effort. And for an A, Grandpa will give you $100," or even "Never draw to an inside straight."

They always listened, appeared interested, and could often recite the stories from memory.

So I started this book to leave lessons for my grandchildren, and family stories. And then I noticed these lessons could offer something to others. And everyone needs a purpose.

AH HA! Everyone could use a good life purpose.

So I dedicate *AH HA!* The Power of Purpose to my most attentive audience, my Grandchildren:

Jocelyn, Amelie, Scout, Lucas, Jackson, Ellie, Owen, and Lily.

And to my wife, Gail, and my children, Allison, Courtney, and Brian, thank you for listening to my stories, usually patiently, even though you have heard them a thousand times.

Read This First

All my public life, I have concluded every speech or presentation with a Town Hall Format, a call for questions or comments. I used to say, "Give me your question and I will fumble around for an answer, or just give me the answer and I will ponder about what the question could have been."

So, if you have any questions, comments, or rebuttal speeches, send them to me at Stevebartlettpurpose@gmail.com

I will read them, ponder them, and send you my answer, or at least a pondering.

Thanks for reading.

AH HA! *The* POWER *of* PURPOSE

FAMILY, FAITH,
and A LIFE WELL-LIVED

Steve Bartlett

Table of Contents

INTRODUCTION

This is somewhat of a memoir, a memoir with a purpose. In each ***AH HA!*** moment, I identify the purpose, and do everything possible to achieve that purpose. Everything.

Much of the story has a backdrop of politics: starting in the sixth grade, then to Young Republicans, in my twenties and thirties as part of the Reagan Revolution, four tumultuous years as mayor of Dallas, and then a stint leading an organization of 100 of the largest financial services in the U.S. Throughout the politics, my family and faith are central to the purpose.

It's also something of a "kiss-and-tell," except everyone who might be offended is dead or has long since laughed it off. I hope.

Rather, this is my collection of stories, *AH HA!* moments of insight. I've added a Life Lesson to each *AH HA!*. In most cases, I laid out the Purpose explicitly. In others, the purpose is embedded in the story.

An *AH HA!* is a moment that delivers an instant encapsulation of what just happened in a single vignette and teaches a quick lesson, small or profound.

As I reflect, my life has gone from one *AH HA!* moment to another. And they all string together in one continuous moment.

I've tried to divide the *AH HA!* moments into segments of my life, although as you'll see, they often blur together.

You will no doubt notice that most of these stories favor me. That's not because I did not make mistakes, miscalculations, and gaffes. I made plenty. But I've either forgotten them or have chosen not to tell them.

I enjoyed writing these *AH HA!*'s and living them. I hope you enjoy reading them.

And I suggest to you, dear Reader, take some time to **identify *your* purpose.**

FAMILY AND EARLY LIFE

Little Red

Steve and second calf, Chipper

It all started with "Little Red." I was five. The family had just moved from Los Angeles to fifteen acres in rural Texas, and my dad brought home our first calf (the first of many). A few days old and nursing from a nursing bucket, it was a red calf (I later identified as a Brangus), thus named "Little Red."

Dad and I put Little Red in the pasture behind the garage in a three-sided shack. Dad turned to me and said, "You're in charge of Little Red."

The next day a Norther blew in with 25-degree temperatures, high winds, and freezing rain. Little Red got sick. I put down fresh hay. Tried to give him milk but he wouldn't eat.

Two days later, Little Red died. I started digging a hole in the pasture to bury Little Red. I admit I only got about six inches from the surface, but Dad finished up when he got home. Neither of us spoke.

At dinner that night, Mother could tell I was sad. "Don't worry about it, Stephen. You did everything you could."

Dad's arm slammed to the table, shaking the plates. "No, you didn't! You didn't change his hay every hour, you didn't clean his diarrhea, you didn't warm his milk and feed him with a milk-soaked rag, you didn't bring him in the house and sleep with him on blankets in front of the stove, you didn't ask your mother to call the vet.

"**If raising Little Red was your purpose, you would have done everything you could**. And Little Red would have lived."

We soon got a second calf, Chipper, and he lived. But I never, *never* forgot the lesson of Little Red.

***AH HA!* Do everything you can to accomplish your purpose. EVERYTHING.**

The Barbed Wire Fence

I was twelve years old and six months into Boy Scouts. I quickly passed Bobcat and Second Class, and First Class was close.

A National Jamboree was announced for Colorado Springs, and several Scouts from our troop were going. The only problem was that it cost $120.

One hundred and twenty dollars! For our family, it might as well have been a million, more than even my mother had in her "selling eggs in town" fund.

She asked my dad. He said no. They argued, often in front of me at dinner.

One Saturday morning after breakfast, Dad said, "Come with me, Son." We walked to the back pasture. There were three old, rusty, dilapidated barbed wire fences. To my twelve-year-old eyes, they looked half a mile long.

Pointing to the fences, Dad said, "I'm going to pay someone $120 to tear down those fences. Roll the wire up tight and stack it here. Pull out the posts and stack 'em here. You want the job?"

"Yes, Sir," I said enthusiastically.

My purpose was to attend the Jamboree. The barbed wire offered the way to get there.

Never a better Jamboree. I've still got the scars.

_AH HA!_ Life is so much better when you earn it _yourself._

Run Rabbit Run

Here is a part of my young life that I don't believe anyone else, except possibly my older sister Pat, knows: I had a speech impediment until the fourth grade. Not a really bad one, but not one I could carry into adulthood. I couldn't pronounce my R's.

So "Run Rabbit Run" came out as baby talk, "Wun Wabbit Wun."

I was vaguely aware that I had to fix this, but didn't know how. More to the point, by the fourth grade, I had an idea that I was meant for important things in life, and the baby talk of "Wun Wabbit Wun" wouldn't cut it.

To that point, when I was in the third grade at a Sunday dinner, my mother and the hostess, Miss Johnny, seated me next to the local state senator because they knew I liked to talk politics.

My mother whispered to Miss Johnny that I was a Republican. Miss Johnny whispered back, "He's not *too* bad, is he?"

My fourth-grade teacher, Mrs. Grigsby, soon noticed my speech impediment and took action. She sent a note home with me to my mother, requesting a teacher conference.

That night at dinner, Mother found her courage and confronted Father: "Mrs. Grigsby wants me to take Stephen to Southwest Texas State Teachers College for tests."

"What for? How much is this going to cost me? What's wrong with the way he talks?"

"Well, I'm taking him," said Mother, holding her ground.

Southwest Texas State, now Texas State University, was the first college campus I had ever seen, and I was impressed. We met with Empress Young Zedler, Ph.D., the director of the Speech Clinic, and easily the smartest person I had ever met.

She put me through a battery of cognitive tests. I didn't know they were called "cognitive" at the time. I just thought they were tests. At the conclusion, she made direct eye contact and said, "Young man, you know the nine planets, the seven continents, the works of Shakespeare, the cause of the Civil War, the details of the Battle of the Bulge, a dozen state capitals, you can name fifteen presidents, and you answered every question I asked. So why can't you pronounce your R's?"

"Nobody ever taught me."

So she taught me where to put my tongue to say "R." It took about fifteen minutes. She then gave me a copy of her book, *Listening for Speech Sounds*, signed *"To my friend Stephen Bartlett."*

My purpose was to speak clearly, for my life in the future.

I still proudly have that book. Thank you, Dr. Zedler, Mrs. Grigsby, and Mother.

***AH HA!* Everybody needs a little help.**

Reach for the Stars

It was early in the sixth grade when the light bulb went off: My destiny was politics. My Social Studies teacher, Mrs. Copeland, was humorless but dedicated to teaching twelve-year-olds about government and politics. As far as I know, I was her only success that year. While my classmates were bored with it, I ate up every word about the bicameral legislature, the three branches of government, and We the People.

Early that year, Mrs. Copeland asked me to stay after class.

"Stephen, you seem to be interested in current events. What magazines do you read at home?"

"*Boy's Life*, *Farm Journal*, *Reader's Digest*, and, when my dad remembers, yesterday's copy of the *San Antonio Express*."

"If I bring you my copy of last week's *U.S. News & World Report* every week, will you read it?"

"Every word, ma'am!"

I didn't really know exactly what *U.S. News & World Report* was, but I could barely contain my excitement just from its title.

That entire year, I did indeed read every issue, cover to cover.

Fast forward to the fall semester of seventh grade. My all-time favorite teacher was Dr. A. L. Weinberger, Assistant Superintendent and Associate Professor at the University of Texas.

He introduced me to Walter Prescott Webb, J. Frank Dobie, *The Great Frontier*, how to truly study history with a long view, and how to write an academic paper. And discipline. And focus. And setting goals. And empathy.

His favorite expression, repeated often, was "Reach for the Stars! You may or may not touch a star, but you won't grab a handful of mud."

He learned my family was moving to Dallas at the end of the semester.

In the cafeteria, he called me over and said, "Sit with me, Mr. Bartlett."

We spoke of many things: politics in Dallas, finding good, sensible friends, setting high goals, bigotry, and so much more. We also talked about reaching for the stars.

Then he said, "Mr. Bartlett, you have something special. You can do anything you set out to do. Go into politics. You can help others. You could be a state senator, or governor, or a U.S. congressman. Use your talents to do good. **Achieve your purpose**."

Thank you, Mrs. Copeland.

Thank you, Dr. Weinberger.

_AH HA!_ Reach for the stars!

A Word about my Siblings

Pat, Steve, Paula, Jeff, Cookie

Pat, Jeff, Cookie, and Paula. We grew up close, and I'm really happy to say we've stayed close for all our lives. Well, almost all our lives, as our brother Jeff dropped out of sight just after our mother died in 2002. No one knows why, but I think it had to do with his new wife, who had an extensive family of her own. My sisters and I miss him.

Of course, it might have been because I was the big brother as we grew up, and no matter what he did, I was always two years ahead of him. And maybe because I teased him constantly, because I could, including stealing his clothes when we were swimming in the creek and making him run home butt naked. Sorry, Jeff.

Pat, or Patricia as she likes to be called, was the big sister, almost a mini-mom. Still is. Always ready with a bowl of popcorn and a batch of fudge when things got tough. Like the night she was babysitting in our parents' absence. Jeff and I headed out after dark, looking for lost sheep. I hated those sheep. Pat called the sheriff, and we came back about midnight. Popcorn was ready.

Cookie, whose real name was Pamela Marie, was the little sister who always hung out with her big brothers, trying to keep up. She actually won the "peeing for distance" contest. I'm not making that up.

Paula, always the kid sister, was the apple of our father's eye. She grew up confident and well-adjusted. Her goal in life was to be a wife and mom, which she accomplished quite well by marrying at age sixteen. She married a steelworker named Eddie. Every Friday, he would present her with his weekly paycheck. If it had sufficient overtime pay, she would kiss him in approval. If not, not.

Pat, Cookie, Paula, I love you guys and am glad we stayed together. And I love you too, Jeff, and miss you. **Growing up with close siblings helps achieve all purposes.**

AH HA! **Family is forever.**

Jump Up My Ass

I was sixteen and the new president of the Dallas County High School Republicans. With twelve hundred members, I was pretty sure I was the cat's meow, the hottest teenage boy ever to come along.

I called my best friend, Wick Allison, president of the Highland Park Young Republicans and the guy who had elected me.

"Wick, we need money to buy some Goldwater yard signs. I'm going to assess your club for one hundred dollars."

"Sure," he said, "but you'll have to ask my treasurer, Gail Coke. Meet me at the Village Camera Store in Highland Park at nine o'clock tomorrow morning."

That seemed easy enough. Too easy, as it turned out.

We showed up at nine o'clock. Wick snapped his fingers loudly and shouted, "Gail, come up here." Even I could tell that was not a good start.

The most beautiful girl I had ever seen, before or since, stormed to the front of the store, eyes flashing fire. She stared at us without speaking.

"Gail, this is Steve Bartlett, president of the Dallas County Federation. He has something to ask you."

I stammered something about yard signs and one hundred dollars.

"Jump up my ass," was all she said before she turned on her heel and stormed off. She never said "hello" or "nice to meet you."

"Wick, I think I'm going to marry that girl."

"That's what I figured."

From that moment, **my purpose was to marry that girl and make her happy**. We have been married fifty-six years as I write this.

***AH HA!* When you fall in love, follow your instincts.**

A Run-in With a Lawn Mower that Changed My Life

Sometimes, a really bad accident is for the good.

In the summer of 1965, I was again mowing lawns to add to my savings account. I was in a hurry to finish mowing the lawn so I could get to a political meeting, as usual.

Long story short, my left foot slipped under the lawnmower. Not pretty: blood, bones, tendons, flesh, big toe, and the ball of my foot in all directions. I put the remains of my foot in my hands and squeezed, convinced the homeowner to drive me to Chester Clinic (we didn't have 911 back then), and thirty days later, I checked out with a cane.

I promptly mowed the front lawn to prove I could, and then threw the cane away. As my purpose was to win a future election, I would not limp.

My dad told me, as I went into surgery, that I would lose my foot. He had lost his leg on a landmine in World War II. So when I woke up and realized it was "only" my toe, I took it as good news.

Gail visited me every single day in the hospital and during my recovery at home. That was a big deal since she lived in University Park and I lived in Oak Cliff. She was forbidden by her mother to ever go to Oak Cliff. I loved that girl before, but those sixty days of daily visits settled it for all time.

But the coda to this episode was still to come. On my eighteenth birthday, I went to the federal courthouse to register for the draft. Then I went down the hall to enlist in the U.S. Army, a family tradition.

The recruiting sergeant, with stripes all the way to his elbow, took one look at me and thought he had struck gold: Boy Scout, "A" student, well-spoken, natural leader. He had me signed up for basic training upon graduation, then radio school, then OCS, and finally Second Lieutenant.

When he learned of my toe amputation, he tore up his extensive plan and ordered me to leave, snarling that an amputation was an automatic 1-Y and I was ineligible to enlist.

Years later, I went back and calculated the sergeant's timeline. I figure I would have arrived in Vietnam as a Second Lieutenant, assigned to a rifle squad thirty days before the start of the Tet Offensive. The odds of surviving would have been slim.

To this day, I believe **the purpose of the lawnmower was God's plan.**

AH HA! Sometimes God's plan just happens.

A Honeymoon Means Out of the Country

Gail and Steve

Summer of 1969. Gail was close to graduation and had gone to Dallas to work and plan our wedding for July 18. I stayed in Austin to work full-time and save enough for the fall semester.

I called three weeks before the wedding at 6:00 p.m., when the rates went down. We could only afford three minutes.

"Sweetheart, I have the honeymoon planned. First night at the Royal Coach Inn in Dallas. Next night at the Brookside Inn in Waxahachie. Then, in Salado at the Stagecoach Inn." These would have been the most expensive hotels I had ever stayed in. "Then the rest of the week relaxing in our little duplex in East Austin. Romantic. Just the two of us."

Icy silence. "Let me explain something, 'Big Boy.' A honeymoon means out of the country. No honeymoon, no wedding. No wedding, no marriage."

"What are you saying?"

"You're a smart boy. You'll figure it out."

"Your three minutes are up." *Click.* Dial tone.

I carefully added up all available resources plus my next two paychecks. Brothers-in-law Mike and Brewer each came through with one hundred dollars cash. Thank you.

Day 1: We stayed at Royal Coach as planned. Dinner was takeout from Jack-in-the-Box, which was all I could afford.

Day 2: At duplex in Austin.

Day 3: Drive to McAllen, where our mutual friend Peggy O'Neal would drive us across the Rio Grande to Reynosa Airport. Catch a propeller airplane to Mexico City. No air ventilation on the tarmac. Oil leaking out of the prop. More passengers than seats. The woman next to me had a grocery sack of chicken heads.

Day 4: Ritz Hotel in Mexico City. Pancho Villa stayed there, and it was old then. Dinner at a saloon next door. June 20, 1969. We were the only gringos in the place just as Neil Armstrong spoke his historic words, "The Eagle has landed." I stood on the bar and made a speech about U.S.–Mexico friendship. Enthusiastic applause from the amigos.

Day 5: Midnight bus to Acapulco (saved a night's hotel). Stopped by bandits with machine guns. My bride put her wedding ring in her mouth and said, "They'll have to dig it out with a knife." I love that woman. Stayed in a hotel three blocks from the beach. Iguanas on the ceiling.

Day 6: Took the nickel bus to La Perla nightclub. Two-dollar cover and two-drink minimum at two dollars each. For each of us. I couldn't even count that high.

So we walked down the jungle path to a Quonset hut where the divers and the locals hung out.

Thunderstorm, sheets of rain, lightning, thunderclaps. Remember, I said *Quonset hut*. The phone rang, and the crowd went silent. "Jose, your turn."

Jose turned white with fear but headed for the door. I turned to my bride. "We can't miss this." She smiled and took my hand.

Into the lightning and sheets of rain. Down the path and up the other side. As we watched, Jose made a perfect swan dive into the Pacific, illuminated by lightning.

And that's when I knew, really knew, I loved this woman.

The next day, we went back to Reynosa and drove to Austin to start our life together.

And that was our purpose.

AH HA! **Don't pass up the good stuff.**

Adam Will Be With Us Forever

Adam

My last full semester at UT. Gail and I were in marital bliss, and with her working full-time, I could finally go to class full-time. I earned twenty-six credit hours that semester.

One big exception to my academic success: Spanish. UT required four semesters of Spanish, and I just could not quite get it, perhaps because the classes were always at 8:00 a.m. So, in my last semester, I was stuck taking fourth-semester Spanish for the third time. Because of Gail, I made it to 8:00 a.m. class this time, but I still struggled.

Two weeks before the end of the semester, the very nice, kind teacher's assistant (TA) announced that he and his wife had kittens looking for good homes. He seemed desperate, and I knew I was not passing and thus couldn't graduate.

So, after class, I told the TA my wife and I were looking for a kitten. I rode my bike to his apartment that afternoon (without telling Gail, of course). All the kittens were black, one with a patch of white under his throat. I named him Adam, as in Adam's apple.

I asked which was his favorite. Adam, of course. I biked home with Adam in my book bag. Gail was thrilled, fortunately.

At the final exam, I brought my paper to the TA and asked him to grade it right then, as I needed this course to graduate.

He graded the exam: D. He then pulled out his grade book with lots of tests and quizzes. He read across: C, F, F, D, C-, B-, F, F, D, F, and so forth. Gulp. My life flashed in front of me.

The TA turned to me and said, "How's Adam?"

"We love Adam. He will be with us forever."

"Looks like a B to me."

My purpose was to graduate from UT. Adam helped me achieve that purpose.

And Adam lived with us for nineteen years. And he has been with us ever since. That black cat seems to pop up at special moments: the birth of our children, Brian's auto wreck, the new house in Washington, driving the girls to boarding school, and even the Rangers' opening game.

AH HA! **You never know where you'll get some good luck.**

Did You Take the GS-12 or the Management Intern?

During the spring semester leading to graduation, I did my job and career search, including letters, interviews, and a few trips to Dallas. Gail, of course, was involved and offered her opinions.

In January, I went to Dallas for final interviews and selection. I narrowed it to three choices: a federal government job starting at GS-12 (note: federal civil service positions are ranked GS-1 through GS-15; GS-12 has a nice salary, benefits, and security); a management internship at Texas Power and Light, with good salary, benefits, and a fast track to executive positions; and a real estate company buying and selling raw land, straight commission, no salary, not even a draw. You eat what you kill.

My purpose was to have an independent source of income and achieve wealth, not a pension.

I got home to Austin in time for dinner prepared by "Her Highness." Steak. Champagne. She was too excited and nervous to ask.

After dinner, she popped the question breathlessly. "What happened?"

I told her I took the straight-commission real estate job. Thud. Tears. She did not pop the champagne.

It's a good thing I made my first sale in four weeks. I used part of my first commission check to buy an oil painting of three Apache warriors sitting in council for $125. The Apaches are still with us, and Gail is still with me.

But it was a long four weeks.

My purpose was to launch a career, not to merely get a job.

***AH HA!* Follow your gut and go for it.**

You Get One Chance to Answer This Question

Our daughter Allison had some challenges as a teenager. Gail and I called it "The Troubles."

Two incidents, of many, come to mind.

During spring break, she stayed with me for a week in Washington. I had a condo on the twelfth floor. Quiet place with mostly older adults. I was heading back to Dallas. She asked if she could stay in D.C. for the weekend with her friend Jerri. "I'll be good, I promise."

When I returned Sunday night, I was met by the condo association with an eviction notice. Seems Allison had hosted the party to end all parties: a heavy metal band, kegs of beer, and plenty of bottles, people hanging by one hand over the balcony, jumping on the hoods of parked cars, and the sheriff was called out multiple times. I had to agree in writing to never allow Allison on the property again.

When I confronted Allison with the evidence and her monumental punishment (six-month grounding, loss of license, no allowance, etc.), I asked, "You knew you'd be caught. Was it worth it?"

"Oh yeah! It was a hell of a party!"

A few months later, we threw in the towel and enrolled her in boarding school in Colorado.

At 4:00 a.m., I got the call from the Farmers Branch Police. "Congressman, we've got your daughter." She had exited her bedroom window at midnight.

Arriving at the police station, she was visibly angry at the "injustice" of being arrested.

I quietly said, "You have one chance to answer my question. Answer it right, and we can go home. Answer it wrong, and the police will book you into Sterrett Jail, with two thousand inmates, and put you into the drunk tank with forty really rough women who will no doubt beat the hell out of you. Ready?"

"Do you want to go home with your mom and me?"

Gulp. Angry glare. Silence. Then, "Y-y-yes."

We left for Colorado, and all was well. Allison grew into a wonderful adult with troubled teens of her own. Serves her right.

My purpose was to help a feisty teenager grow into a mature young woman.

AH HA! Raising Teens is not for the faint of heart. Stay calm.

Dad, Do You Know What They Do to North Dallas Girls in West Dallas?

Allison's younger sister, Courtney, was no Sunday School teacher. One story stands out among many.

She attended a really fine, expensive middle school, the Episcopal School of Dallas. In the spring of eighth grade, she was failing every single subject.

At dinner one evening, she announced, "Dad, you know I'm failing the eighth grade."

"Your mother has told me."

"But don't worry, Episcopal School has a really fun summer school."

"You won't be going there. You'll be catching the school bus to Pinkston in West Dallas." Pinkston was adjacent to thirty-five hundred public housing units with the highest crime rate in Dallas.

"Dad, do you know what they do to North Dallas blonde girls in West Dallas?"

"I hear it's pretty rough. But that's where you're going."

Turning pale, she left the table to start studying. She passed, barely.

Her purpose was to stay out of West Dallas.

The next year, we also sent her to boarding school.

***AH HA!* Proper motivation is the secret.**

Mom, Dad Left Us!

One more for both of the daughters.

They both smoked cigarettes as teenagers. We disapproved, scolded, punished, argued, and threatened. All the usual parent reactions.

Finally, we remembered a core tenet of parent training: "Don't try to control your teens. Control yourself."

So, Gail and I sat down with them and calmly stated, "We know you smoke. We don't approve, but it's your business. But from this moment, your mother and I will never again be present with anyone, other than our parents, while they are smoking."

The following Sunday, I invited the girls to lunch at El Chico, about a mile and a quarter away. It was a cold, windy day, and I noted that they didn't wear coats.

After lunch, Courtney "lit up." I didn't say anything. Just stood up as if going to the men's room. Handed the cashier $20 on the way out, got in my car, and drove home.

As I walked in the front door, I heard Gail on the phone with the girls wailing, "Mom, Dad left us! It's cold. How are we going to get home?"

Gail calmly replied, "I don't know, and don't really care. Have a nice walk."

They came shivering about thirty minutes later. Spoke not a word.

Neither ever "lit up" in front of me again. Ever. And they quit cigarettes a few years later. **And that was my purpose.**

AH HA! **Control yourself, not other people.**

Mother's Dog Died

Early in our marriage, I invested as a silent partner in a BBQ restaurant in San Antonio. The first summer, my business partner Steve Spence called to say he had a week of Army Reserve duty and asked if I could watch the restaurant in his absence. I wouldn't have to do anything, just greet the customers, watch the money, and close up.

Piece of cake, I thought. Wrong.

I landed Friday morning. Friday and Saturday nights were busy, but no sweat.

Then came Sunday night. By 7:00 p.m., the cook had passed out drunk on the woodpile, the lead waitress was a no-show, the number two waitress walked off the job when the busboy groped her, and it was the first night for the number three waitress. We were slammed with a couple of large parties at once.

I was the cook, slicing BBQ and preparing plates in the kitchen, with all hell breaking loose in the dining room. The wall phone rang.

As I was slicing the meat, I answered, "Settlement Inn."

It was Gail, sobbing hysterically. "Mother's dog died! *(Sob, sniffle).* Can you come home?"

Saying not a word, I hung up the phone and continued preparing food. Eventually, the cook woke up, and waitress number one showed up.

I forgot all about the dog.

The following Friday night, I arrived home. Put the key in the front door. The locks had been changed. Oh God… *her mother's dog.*

I carefully rang the doorbell. Gail greeted me with a big wet kiss, a glass of bourbon, and a candlelight dinner. I waited for the explosion.

After dinner, I quietly said, "Darling, I am so sorry about your mother's dog."

"Oh, thank you for caring. It was pretty rough at first, but we got through it."

"I couldn't help but notice the locks have been changed."

"Oh, that? I lost my keys in the shopping center parking lot and had the locks changed. Why do you ask?"

"Oh, no reason."

My purpose at that moment was to keep a *happy wife.* And I almost missed it.

AH HA! **Never assume she's angry unless she tells you. And pay attention to her mother's dog.**

I'm Aware of Where Steve is From, and We Shall Not Speak of It Again

And speaking of Gail's mother, bless her heart, she did not approve of me. Never hostile or even harsh words, but I was from Oak Cliff, the wrong side of town, across the river, working class on a good day. Our home was about the size of Gail's living and dining room.

One Christmas, we had Christmas dinner at the home of Gail's sister. Somehow, the name "Oak Cliff" was mentioned in passing. Gail's older sister, who had accepted me into the family after I got elected to Congress, stated, "Well, Mom, you know that Steve is from Oak Cliff." The table got cold and dead quiet.

Gail's mother arched her right eyebrow so violently that it jiggled her wig.

"I am aware of that fact. And we shall not speak of it again."

And we never did.

My purpose was to stay in the good graces of Gail's family.

AH HA! **It matters to some where you're from.**

I Think I Can Do Better Than That by Myself

And then there is my son Brian. True confession: Brian and I did not get along very well during his teenage years and early twenties. We are way better now, and I accept full responsibility for our difficulties. My bad.

Late in his senior year, I was at my office when Brian called around 10:30 a.m. Gravelly teenage-boy, just-woke-up voice. Gail was out of town.

"Dad, I overslept and missed a final exam. If I get a zero on the exam, I will fail the course and flunk out. No diploma, no college. Can you call the school and handle it?"

"Happy to. You got the phone number for the school?"

"Oh, good. It's 972-471-22… uh, wait, that was too easy. What are you going to say?"

"I'm going to say you stayed up all night playing video games and overslept."

"Dad, I think I can do better than that myself. Uh, do you know how I can reach Mom?"

"No, I don't. Got anything else for me? I'm kinda busy."

My purpose was to help Brian find his way.

AH HA! **Be careful who you ask for help.**

Dad's Gonna Kill Brian or Brian's Going to Kill Dad

Two years later, we went on a family ski vacation at our cabin in New Mexico. Brian had brought his girlfriend and was trying to impress her. I regret to say I was being a jerk. Brian and I had been circling and sniffing around each other like two dogs looking for a fight.

On the third day, at 7:30 a.m., I encountered Brian in the living room. He said something, and I escalated (I said I regret it). Within minutes, we were nose to nose, eyes fixed in rage, fists clenched.

"Take your best shot."

"You first."

"No, you try it."

At that moment, I heard Courtney running upstairs. "Allison, come quick. Dad's gonna kill Brian, or Brian's gonna kill Dad. I don't know which, but it's gonna be really cool."

That broke the spell for me. I realized I was supposed to be the adult. I averted my eyes, unclenched my fists, and slowly backed away.

That's when I realized **my purpose was to take responsibility as a father.** It took me a while to act on that.

***AH HA!* Be the adult.**

The New Zealand Trek: "This isn't going to work, Dad."

Fast forward four years. Brian is twenty-four, and we still don't have a working relationship. We both thought, or maybe hoped, that a trek in New Zealand's South Island would help us get it together.

The first three days weren't going so well. I was giving him advice he didn't want. Again, my bad.

On the morning of the third day, we were camped on the ground with no tent. The sun was just coming up. I woke up to see Brian with his backpack fully packed, glaring down at me.

"Dad, this isn't going to work."

He turned and walked away, up the valley.

Stunned, I began sorting through the "what should I do" list, weighing all the options. Then I realized I didn't have to do anything. He was an adult. His plane ticket home was in his pocket. And he was right.

It was going to be a much better trek for both of us.

And that's when I grew up and started thinking of Brian as an adult. A noble purpose

We reconciled six months later, and things have been better ever since.

_AH HA!_ A solo trek in New Zealand can clear your head.

Eight Hugs

Like most families, ours has its own traditions. Some are small, like seated dinners at the dining room table. Some are big, like an insistence on annual vacations.

As an aside, when Allison was seventeen and still in her "troubles," I commented that this would be the last time we were all together on vacation. She bristled and demanded, "Why?" I replied, "Well, you've always said that when you turn eighteen, we will never see you again."

"Well, I can still come on the family vacation, can't I?" As I write this, she is fifty-three and has never missed a family vacation.

But the biggest family tradition, unique to the Bartlett family, is Eight Hugs.

The rule is that if anyone is grumpy or out of sorts, any family member can call out, "Eight Hugs!" All family members at once descend on the grump and engage in a group hug, chanting, "1, 2, 3, 4, 5, 6, 7, 8." If the offending party does not put on a smile, we hug to eight again, and again if necessary.

No one has ever survived as grumpy for more than three collective Eight Hugs.

Now the grandchildren are part of it, and the youngest ones love to call "Eight Hugs!" at the first hint of a frown.

My purpose was to lighten the mood and achieve a loving family.

_AH HA!_ You can cure any dispute with a good hug.

I'm Sorry, Dad

My Dad is on the right. I'm on the left

This one is about family, but it occurred way, way later in life, about sixty years later.

And I am not proud of it.

My dad was what you could call a tough old bird, and some would call him worse. He was the classic World War II vet. He stepped on a land mine in the Battle of Hürtgen Forest in the German-Belgium border region on November 5, 1944. (Most people don't know about the Hürtgen, but it was both the longest infantry battle in U.S. history and one of the worst failures, so it is rarely mentioned.)

I digress. My dad was tough, and he expected all his family to be tough. A strict disciplinarian. And he only had to speak once. Growing up, I woke up every morning to the sound of his wooden leg marching up the hallway toward my room. I was expected to be up and at attention before he opened the door.

On the weekends, he literally built, with hammer and nails, our four-bedroom house with his own two hands. My job was to carry stuff, a lot of stuff. He never complained. Neither did I.

The only time I almost detected a slight catch in his voice was when he came into my hospital room after the lawnmower accident to tell me the doctor said he was going to amputate my foot. (As it turned out, the surgeon was able to save two-thirds of my foot.) He said, matter-of-factly, "Don't want you to be surprised when you wake up. The doc said he's going to take off your foot when you go into surgery. I'll tell your mother." I replied, "I figured. Thanks for telling me."

I accepted him for what he was. I never expected or delivered tenderness. I loved him, no doubt, but it was not a warm and fuzzy love.

He developed lung cancer in his seventies. It was a long, slow process, but he never complained, and I never expressed sympathy. I took care of business, helping to find home health care and managing his budget with Mom. I gave the eulogy, focusing on his strong discipline.

In my heart, I suppose I knew I should go to him, tell him I loved him, and have that talk about how much he meant to me, and thank him for all he taught me.

I meant to, but somehow, I just couldn't. Our relationship was respect, discipline, teaching toughness, getting the job done, man to man, not sentimental.

I wish I had.

I lost my purpose.

AH HA! **I'm sorry, Dad.**

PRELUDE: YOUNG REPUBLICANS

We Don't Have Any Republicans in That Part of Town!

Summer before my junior year of high school. I had been at Kimball High School for a year but hadn't found my niche. I was absorbed in politics, but only as an observer. I had read Barry Goldwater's books and attended, as a guest, the Republican State Convention to hear him speak. I was hooked.

I decided to join the Young Republicans, but only after the Republican Party nominated my hero, Barry Goldwater. I was mowing lawns that summer, but I took off every afternoon that week to watch the convention.

The minute Barry Goldwater was nominated, I picked up the telephone and dialed Dallas County Republican Headquarters.

"Hello, my name is Steve Bartlett, and I want to join the Young Republicans."

"What school do you go to?"

"Kimball, in Oak Cliff."

"We don't have any Republicans in that part of town." *Click.* Dial tone.

I called a few friends whom I knew to be sympathetic. (One was Larry Stansberry, who went on to become Chair of Pediatrics at Columbia University.) We met that night and adopted the bylaws I drafted on my

1935 manual typewriter. Collected two dollars each in dues. Elected myself president.

The next morning, I called headquarters again and told them I now had a club with five dues-paying members.

"Too small," said the person answering the phone.

Took me five days. I called again.

"We now have a club with forty-two dues-paying members. Where do I get some Goldwater yard signs?"

"You now have the largest Young Republican Club in Dallas County. When can you come to headquarters?"

I got there by 2:00 p.m. via city bus. Met the Young Republican president, Wick Allison. He claimed he had forty-three members. We became best friends and instant allies.

And my political career was launched. **And that was my purpose**.

AH HA! **Doesn't matter where you're from. It's where you're going. And it helps to be president of the largest club.**

John Tower and Winning Elections

As I said, Barry Goldwater was my political hero, and the 1964 Goldwater campaign was my first campaign. I was indeed a true believer.

After Goldwater and the entire Republican Party went down in flames, I was not at all discouraged. From where I stood, the true conservative movement had not lost but had won 27 million votes, more than any true conservative presidential candidate had ever received.

I even made tie tacks and lapel pins highlighting a big bold *"27"* and passed them out to my friends, who proudly displayed them.

That was in November. In December, Senator John Tower, a true-blue conservative, called a leadership meeting in Dallas. I was invited on behalf of the Young Republicans. A cold, rainy night at the Executive Inn across from Love Field. Two hundred Republican leaders, by invitation only, showed up to get our marching orders from the great John Tower himself.

He stood before us, hands on his hips.

"Friends, you know me. No one is more conservative than I. Like you, I gave this campaign everything I had. *Everything!*

"But today, only three elected Republicans are left in the entire state of Texas.

"And if we don't change our approach, after the next election, there will be none.

"So, we must change. Not our principles, but the way we describe our message. We must be kinder, more sympathetic, willing to compromise, inviting the vast majority into our party, excluding no one, asking the public to join us, and all with a smile.

"And time is short. We must start tonight."

With that, he slowly pointed at the crowd from front to back, from right to left, and back again.

"If there is anyone in here who is not willing to follow me and change the way we deliver our message, *leave now.*"

No one moved. No one left. Some forgot to breathe.

"Good. Now let's get to work."

The rest of the meeting, lasting well into the night, was a planning session with a new approach, new energy, and a new inviting attitude: asking every Texan to join us and listening to what they had to say. Our purpose was to win elections, starting now.

That was December 10, 1965. Twenty-three months later, in November 1966, John Tower was re-elected handily; multiple Republican candidates were elected throughout the state, including George Bush to Congress in Houston. A year later, in 1967, my predecessor Jim Collins was elected to Congress from Dallas.

The purpose was to create a majority party.

***AH HA!* You get more votes with a smile and an open mind than a scowl and a closed fist.**

Know the Rules

Back to Young Republicans, my training ground.

My two best friends, Wick Allison and Jim Oberwetter, often said, "Everything I know about politics I learned in Young Republicans." I met Jim in my first semester at UT, and he, Wick, and I became inseparable.

The first thing to learn is to know the rules. Follow the rules. Make them work for you.

For example, conventions often have a "Unit Rule." That means if two-thirds of a delegation votes one way, all the votes are cast that way.

In 1967, I was a candidate for First Vice Chairman of the State Young Republicans. There were twelve hundred delegates in total, and it was close. My vote count showed me about fifteen votes behind.

Solution: I had some support at UT, but less than the required one-third to break the Unit Rule. The rule said "two-thirds of the votes present." Jim Oberwetter identified seven Bartlett supporters who were unwilling to vote for me but didn't want to vote for my opponent. He quietly got them off the convention floor, locked them in a hotel room, and said, "Stay here until the voting is over." It broke the Unit Rule, and I picked up fifteen votes from UT.

I won First Vice Chairman and later Chairman. My opponent, who had grand plans, was never heard from again.

In 1969, my last year as Chairman, a big election for national chairman was being held in Washington, D.C., on the same day as the Texas Convention. The Rule said Texas votes were to be cast by the State Chairman as of 6:00 p.m. Eastern Time and could be cast by proxy. The Chairman-elect favored one candidate, and I favored another.

No problem. I sent Jim Oberwetter to the National Caucus with my proxy. I kept an open telephone at the podium. Multiple points of order and appeals of the Chair's decisions. Each one required a time-consuming roll call vote.

At 5:17 p.m. Central Time, which was 6:17 p.m. Eastern Time, my successor was elected. Too late. My national candidate was elected seventeen minutes earlier, simply by knowing Central Time is an hour earlier than Eastern Time.

In this case, my only purpose was to prove I could, and leave a lasting impression.

AH HA! **Know the rules. The rules will set you free.**

MOVING TO THE BIGS: DALLAS CITY COUNCIL

A Solid Foundation: Founding Meridian

Gail and I moved to Dallas the first weekend in June 1971. Graduation at UT on Saturday night. The Chairman of UT Regents showed up, stumbling drunk, and had to be escorted from the platform.

On Sunday morning, we loaded up the U-Haul and headed north on I-35.

Monday at 7:30 a.m., I showed up for work at Wilson Properties. Straight commission selling real estate. Did well, but by 1974 the real estate market had crashed, so I had to move on.

That's when I needed to focus on my mission: find a business that would support me while I pursued politics.

Commission work was out. If you were in the middle of a real estate deal, you couldn't stop for a political meeting.

Likewise, a straight salary was out: employers expect you to be at work every day.

And I knew I didn't want to be "kept" on some rich guy's payroll, because then I would be beholden.

So I went to the library and read every business magazine, looking for ideas. Made a list of one hundred possibilities: a radio station, real estate development, fixing up rental houses. Even buying a chain of liquor stores.

I chose injection-molded plastics. Making components for other companies' products. Highly repetitive. Once I get a customer, set up the machinery, and hire operators, I would be free to go to political meetings. More complicated than that, of course, but that's the idea.

Bought the equipment on credit, retained a consultant to teach me how to operate it, and hired a general manager. Jim Foxx, forty years in the industry, and other employers thought him too old. I made him a minority partner on a handshake, and we were in business.

By 1975, I was free to achieve my purpose: to do politics on my own time and business as required. I called it *Meridian Products.* It helped support me through twenty-five years of politics. Remember, being mayor was a more-than-full-time job that paid $50 a week. Jim bought me out in 1999 when I went back to Washington. I think he was glad to get rid of me, but we had a great partnership.

It was neither simple nor easy, but I focused on the goal and made it work.

My purpose was to own a business that would support my political passion. Meridian accomplished that purpose.

AH HA! **Identify your mission and shape your life to achieve it.**

AH HA! Feed His Sheep

So there I was, ready to launch my political career in the adult world. I had a beautiful and totally committed wife, Gail, a new baby, Allison, a home in North Dallas, a business, and an ever-expanding cadre of like-minded friends, loyal to one another, and a commitment to public service.

But my concept of public service was still, to put it bluntly, somewhat fuzzy. Kind of, "get elected and then, then, oh I don't know, get elected again."

And my spiritual life was shallow and not connected to public service.

Early on, Gail and I joined Westminster Presbyterian Church. Large enough to be meaningful, small enough to know everyone in it, family-friendly, nice people, and an hour fellowship after the worship service.

But I confess with some embarrassment, we joined not to find the Lord, but because it was necessary for a political career. But the friends we met there stayed with us all our lives.

Then, after about a year, it happened. The Pastor Emeritus Walter Bennett preached one Sunday. Wise, gentle, kind, soft-spoken.

His message was powerful, but delivered softly. With gentleness.

Jesus asked Peter (John 21:15–17, NLT), *"Do you love me?"*

"Yes, Lord, you know I love you."

"Then feed my sheep."

A revelation! As powerful as Paul on the road to Damascus. (Glad I didn't go blind.)

Twenty years later, when I was mayor, I had occasion to meet Mother Teresa, the Mother Teresa. She did not come to City Hall, but I went to her at a small church in Oak Cliff. After the service, I approached her to welcome her to Dallas.

She clutched my hand in the firmest, warmest handshake I had ever experienced. Looking directly into my eyes, she said clearly, "Mayor, take care of His people."

Pretty similar to "feed His sheep."

My life in politics had a spiritual purpose. If I loved Jesus, I must feed His sheep.

There are many ways to feed His sheep: the ministry, teaching, hunger pantries, and Bible studies.

But I knew my way was politics. Politics is public service; it is feeding His sheep.

I didn't pound the Bible or campaign on my religion, but for the next fifty years, I tried to feed His sheep through politics.

Feed His sheep is a pretty good purpose for all of us.

AH HA! **If you love Him, then feed His sheep.**

Betty, You Left Your Shoes Under My Bed

Now, don't panic and jump to the wrong conclusions.

There I was, age twenty-two, back in Dallas in 1971 with a wife, soon a baby, a starter home in Republican North Dallas, and a successful business.

I knew I wanted to find an office I could win. I knew not to be too pushy or obvious. So my strategy was to simply show up. Be there at gatherings and offer to help. Make friends, get there early.

I helped the precinct chairman and canvassed half the voters for him. Put up and took down the chairs at headquarters. Organized an ice cream party for our block. Joined an Arts group called "500 Inc." Made friends, talked politics, listened to everyone's views.

And I kept a list of names, addresses, and phone numbers of everyone I met. Not exactly a list, but a shoebox with index cards, neat, and alphabetized.

When we moved into our new home, we hosted an open house and invited everyone, and I mean *everyone* in this shoebox of a space, roughly 500 people. About 150 to 200 showed up and spilled into the front yard.

I also went to every Republican meeting and convention possible as a delegate.

I was the new kid, younger than everyone else. Friendly and interested in everyone I met. Never asking for anything.

The first State GOP Convention was in 1972. Houston, I think. First night after all the receptions and caucuses, I found myself with a group of five or six "older women," meaning middle-aged. I suppose I was kind of their mascot. So, I invited them to my room to continue talking about Republican politics.

We were so engrossed in political stories that no one noticed we had been there all night until the sun came up.

The ladies left sheepishly, promising never to tell a soul. One in particular, Betty, older than the others, had taken her shoes off and left barefoot.

I couldn't help myself. At 10:00 a.m., when the convention started, I spotted Betty sitting in the middle of a crowded section. I conspicuously waded across the row of delegates, shoes in hand.

Loudly, I proclaimed, "BETTY, YOU LEFT YOUR SHOES UNDER MY BED WHEN YOU LEFT THIS MORNING." Total silence from the 200 people who heard. Then uproarious laughter.

Talk about a bonding experience. Those women formed the core of my volunteers when I ran for city council.

My purpose was to win friends and support in the Republican grassroots.

AH HA! **Make friends. Lots of them.**

Republican Men's Club? Just Say Yes

Republicans' Men's Club with President Reagan

It was 1974, the summer of the Watergate hearings. Republicans on the ropes. I was twenty-four. A businessman with a family, active in Dallas County Republican politics, but still thought of as "The Kid."

I got a call from Jim Jackson, executive director of the Dallas County Party.

"Can you come over this afternoon? About 4:00."

He handed me five typed pages labeled "Bylaws of Dallas County Republican Men's Club."

"Bob Porter (the chairman and later a federal judge) wants you to be the president of the Men's Club. It was disbanded in 1968, and we can't get anyone else to do it."

"Any members? Treasury? Officers? Minutes?"

"Nope. Nope. Nope. Nope. These aren't even the official bylaws. I just found a form in the library and copied it."

The Watergate hearings would start in about a month. Stunned, I mumbled that I'd think about it.

I walked outside, around the corner to a pay phone at the liquor store, to call my best friend, Wick Allison.

He didn't hesitate. "Walk back inside and accept his offer. Be sure you get all copies of his bylaws so you can write them the way you want them. And say thank you."

I did exactly that. Thirty days later we had our first meeting with 150 members. A luncheon with a speaker. Adopted the new bylaws, elected the officers, including me as president, and collected $500 in dues. We had monthly meetings without fail, and in many ways the Club became the face of the Republican Party.

My purpose was to establish myself as a leader, at least among Republicans.

AH HA!* When you see an opportunity, *carpe diem.

Why Don't *You* Run?

City council campaign headquarters at home.

In 1975, I considered running for an at-large seat on the Dallas City Council. My friends (Wick and Jim and a few more by then) were clear: You can run, but you can't win. So I did not run.

Fast forward to September 1977. Adlene Harrison, the at-large councilwoman I would have run against and lost, suddenly resigned to take the position as regional director of the EPA. The same friends and I huddled and concluded that the downtown establishment would want no part of me. And they told me so.

So, we met every night to identify a downtown candidate we could support. For five days we identified new candidates, and I called each one. Each one turned me down over the phone with various lame excuses that all were the same: Dallas City Council was beneath their station in life.

On day six at the breakfast table, I was whining about the scarcity of patriotism among the City Fathers, hiding behind the newspaper and complaining out loud.

Suddenly, a big, angry hand crushed the newspaper I was holding. It was my sweet wife, Gail, with fire in her eyes:

"If you're so damn patriotic, stop whining and you run!!!"

I think I will. My five friends and I met that morning, and by noon, we had a campaign plan. The aforementioned best friend, Jim Oberwetter, called to say, "Last time you couldn't win. This time, I'm not saying you will win, but you could. When the brass ring comes around, you've got to grab it." *Carpe Diem* again.

I announced two days later and had 200 supporters at my home (I always made sure we had a large house for just such an occasion) that night to launch the campaign.

My purpose was to win elected office.

_AH HA!_ Listen to your spouse. And _carpe diem._

Dallas News Loading Dock

At the time, Dallas was a "3-D" city: Democrat, Downtown establishment, and Dallas Morning News. Things were changing, but I didn't know how fast.

Since I was not a Democrat, I ran as an Independent. When my six Democratic opponents accused me of actually being a Republican, I answered, "I'm also a Presbyterian, a husband, a father, and a small businessman."

When the subject of the Downtown establishment came up, I simply said there should be at least one independent voice on the city council.

Regarding *The Dallas Morning News*, I got lucky. I said all the right things and embraced a few sacred cows (city manager government, AAA bond rating, support for the police, Fair Park) during the editorial board interview. But the best I could hope for was a one-sentence favorable mention as they endorsed my opponent.

Then lightning struck: the long-time editorial director, Dick West, who ruled with an iron hand and disliked change, young whippersnappers, and Republicans, decided to retire. He booked a month-long vacation on Padre Island and left the editorial board to handle things in his absence. The five of them decided to risk their careers and endorse this young, independent, non-establishment Republican.

They wisely kept it a secret until the Sunday edition two weeks out.

As was the political habit back then, I drove to the loading dock of *The Dallas Morning News* as the papers were being loaded at 11:45 p.m. I bought a paper from one end of the dock, and… drum roll please… they not only endorsed me with a *"Bartlett for Council"* headline, but I was the lead editorial.

Trying to catch my breath, I called Wick and Jim from a pay phone. Jim insisted it was a trick and made me drive to the other end of the loading dock and buy another paper to verify.

If your purpose is to win an election in Dallas, an endorsement from *The Dallas Morning News* is a pretty good start.

***AH HA!* Do everything you can, and sometimes you get lucky.**

Don't Predict Your Win *Before* Your Win

With seven candidates and a majority required to win, it was always going to be a runoff. Jim, Wick, and I knew that, but for some reason my main opponent, Pete Baldwin, did not. (Pete was a true gentleman and a fine person.)

On election night for the first round, we celebrated with 200 supporters in our home. I told everyone to expect a runoff and had already made plans for the runoff campaign. My party was, in a word, jubilant.

At one point, my five-year-old daughter Allison pulled on my arm and insisted I pick her up and carry her around the crowd with both of us laughing and waving, and thanking people. After about fifteen minutes, she said, "Put me down."

I asked what that was all about, and she said, "There was a Dallas Morning News photographer following you, and I wanted him to see you looking happy. He's gone now."

My Dallas News photo the next morning showed Allison and her dad laughing and waving at supporters.

Not so my opponent. His photo at his "party" showed him with a really dour look, talking quietly into the telephone. Tag Lines: "Bartlett elated" and "Baldwin disappointed." And those photos were worth a thousand words. Maybe 10,000.

We had each received virtually the same number of votes. But starting with that photo, I went on to win the runoff.

My purpose was to win the runoff, not to just show up well.

AH HA! **Don't count your votes until the election is over, and listen to your daughter.**

Doing Your Homework

I did have a good term on the council. Not perfect, and I made mistakes, mainly by being brash and arrogant.

But I was known to do my homework, learn the subjects in detail, show up in every part of the city, and be willing to take on the tough assignments.

Tough assignments included affordable housing, property tax valuation scandal, the now ubiquitous homestead exemption, creation of the Dallas Arts District, two bond elections, public transportation for disabled riders, our first cable franchise, and Use of Force Rules for Law Enforcement, to name a few. I was sought out for media interviews because reporters knew I would know the subject matter. And I was always available.

Doing my homework was the basis for that. My first council meeting started the morning after my election. I received the four-inch thick council packet about 11:00 p.m., stayed up reading it until 2:00 a.m., and was ready.

One item caught my eye: a requested sidewalk waiver for a new subdivision. It was on the 120-item consent agenda, which was approved on a voice vote.

"I request a one-week hold on Item 78." (Remember my chapter on knowing the rules?)

Dead silence around the council chamber.

"Why? It's routine."

"I'd simply like more information."

During that week, I discovered that waivers for sidewalks were, in fact, routine. And the attorney requesting the waiver was the mayor's best friend. When I asked why we would require sidewalks in the building code and then waive the requirement upon request, no one had an answer. The attorney said, "No one wants sidewalks anymore." I knew that was not true, but I also could tell I was not going to prevail. I decided to simply say, "I don't think this is a good idea. People want sidewalks," and vote no.

The morning of the next council meeting, a small news story appeared in the *Dallas News* about a ten-year-old who had been struck while riding his bike in the subdivision *next door to this waiver request* and was in the hospital with a broken leg. And guess what, no sidewalks.

I placed a copy of the story at each desk. When the item came up, the rest of the council waited in line to make the motion to deny the sidewalk waiver. And there were no more sidewalk waivers for the next three years.

That's when I realized it wasn't about sidewalk waivers; it was about doing your homework. **Be the best city councilman you can be. Not a bad purpose.**

_AH HA!_ Know more about the subject than anyone else.

The Lunch Bunch

I scheduled a regular Saturday 10:00 a.m. to 1:00 p.m. homework session at Andrew's Restaurant, owned by friends Andy and Randy Clendenan, on McKinney Avenue, and studied every item on next week's agenda. This three-hour study time was followed by a 1:00 p.m. lunch with Wick, Jim, Enid, and other friends, later referred to as "The Lunch Bunch."

The Lunch Bunch met every Saturday at 1:00 p.m. My campaign manager, Enid Gray, was the Chair and she ruled with an iron hand. Included in the group over time were Jim Oberwetter, County and then State Republican Party Chairman Fred Meyer, Federal Judge Ed Kinkeade, County Judge Lee Jackson, George W. Bush confidants Karen Hughes and Jeanne Johnson, former Congressman Alan Steelman, White House General Counsel for George W. Bush Harriet Miers and former City Councilman Dick Smith, EPA Regional Administrator Buck Wynne, Enid's driver and friend Randy Stephenson, and occasionally someone who passed Enid's rigorous standards.

No one was allowed to speak unless they had something important to say. Gail was always invited, occasionally attended, but never spoke. Enid once forcefully ejected the State GOP General Counsel because he didn't meet her test. Her exact words were, "This is *my* table. Get out!"

The Lunch Bunch met every Saturday for those in town until sometime in about 2012. Added much knowledge and understanding to the body of Republican knowledge.

You cannot achieve any purpose by yourself.

Those who are still living continue to meet as The Lunch Bunch about once a year.

_AH HA!_ If you don't have something to say, don't say it.

Say Something, Tom!

Dallas had an independent transit agency named DART, for Dallas Area Rapid Transit Agency. DART had created a paratransit to serve people with disabilities. A noble idea, but the problem was in the implementation.

It seems DART's paratransit required an appointment, and the pickup time was a four-hour window. Meaning one could not use it for employment. ("Hey boss, I'll be at work sometime between 6:00 a.m. and 10:00 am.")

I took it as a cause to correct, and was getting little traction. But I was trying, and confident I would succeed.

About that time the local PBS station, Channel 13, invited me to appear on their nightly news. Little did I know I was being set up.

I arrived to discover a friend of mine named Rick Amber was also a guest. Rick used a wheelchair and was a disability activist.

The producer came into the Green Room and asked Rick to come with him to the studio. Curious, I followed.

When we got on set, the host, Tom Grimes, started by showing us a taped video showing the horrors of DART's paratransit operations: people left stranded on the sidewalk for four hours, others missing their dialysis appointments, and so forth. It was an ambush.

Tom turned to me, "Well, Councilman, is the City of Dallas just incompetent or pure evil?"

I rose to the occasion. "Tom, as you can see, my friend Rick here (pointing to the wheelchair) uses a wheelchair. To get into this studio, Rick had to exit the back door, push through the snow to the loading dock, have your people lift him and his chair onto the loading dock, then lift his chair over the various cables.

"So, Tom, is Channel 13 just incompetent or pure evil?"

Tom stared at me for a full minute. Neither of us spoke. I could hear his producer shouting into his earpiece, "Say something, Tom, say something!!!"

Finally, Tom quietly said, "Well, let's just move along," and we proceeded to have a pleasant conversation about how to fix the problem.

And we did fix DART's paratransit operations to pick up and return on time so people could get to work.

And that was the purpose.

_AH HA!_ If you live in a glass house, don't throw stones. At least not on live TV.

Carole Young: "What Are YOU Going To Do About It?"

Two years on the council. Sunday morning at Westminster Presbyterian Church. Fellowship hour, a Presbyterian tradition.

Carole Young was a young homemaker and mother of two. Until this moment, the sweetest, softest spoken person at Westminster, but now she approached me with a look I had never seen from Carole: fear, anger, frustration.

"STEVE, WHAT ARE YOU GOING TO DO ABOUT CRIME IN THIS CITY? It's out of control and you've got to stop it!!!!"

Whew. Carole had never expressed an opinion about any subject. Not knowing what to say, I asked, "Carole, obviously you have something on your mind."

It spewed out in a rush of words: "I was kidnapped and attacked!! Right there in the Valley View Shopping Center parking lot. Held with a knife to my throat while this criminal drove me around for two hours. I cried, I begged, I pleaded. He finally took pity and let me go.

"So, Mr. Councilman, we elected you to stop crime in this city. What are you going to do about it?!!!"

Taking a deep breath, I decided not to be political but to tell her the truth.

"Carole, to answer your question, I am doing everything I know how to lower crime in Dallas. I can give you a list, but you wouldn't believe it. I spend many hours every week trying to make things better.

"But the real question is, *what are you going to do about it?* You live in this city, too. I've done a lot. What are you going to do?"

Carole blinked and walked away. I figured I had just lost her vote forever.

The next Sunday, Carole approached me again. Still angry, but somewhat subdued.

"I hated you all week. Really hated you. Then I realized I couldn't answer your question. So tell me what you meant. I'm a private citizen. What can I do?"

So I told her, "Use your voice, your time, your energy, your passion. I will help you, but it's got to be you. Join the Chamber of Commerce and the Public Safety Committee. Make an appointment with the deputy chief of police. Meet with the Valley View manager, and then the other regional shopping centers. Form a committee of concerned mothers. Make a plan and demand that your plan be adopted. And don't give up."

"I will help you and go with you. But it's your story and you've got to tell it."

She did exactly that.

A year later, we had lighting and patrols in shopping center parking lots, and crime in those lots was down by 40 percent. Over the next thirty years, she went on to chair the Chamber of Commerce, then the North Texas

Crime Commission, advocate for criminal justice in the Legislature, and eventually became Chair of the Texas Board of Criminal Justice. She was regarded as one of the leading voices in Texas for public safety.

I thought my purpose was to reduce crime. **Turns out the purpose was to inspire Carole Young.**

AH HA! **What are *you* going to do about it?**

Have a Plan

In 1979, about 5:00 p.m. I received a call from Jim Frances, Chief of Staff for Governor Bill Clements. Jim was a friend and a political colleague, although we were not close.

"Steve, the governor wants to appoint you to a state commission, the Texas Commission on Intergovernmental Affairs."

"Huh, sounds like a bullshit commission to me."

"No, seriously, the governor has asked for you specifically. But I have to announce it right now. I'm on deadline."

"Well, uh, uh, ok if the governor wants me to."

Now, while Jim was a friend, I knew he had an angle, but I didn't know what it was.

I soon learned the angle. Three days later, *The Dallas Morning News* announced that funding for my commission and a half dozen others had been vetoed by the governor.

I got right on the phone with my friend. "Jim, what the hell is going on? The governor didn't really ask for me, did he?"

"Well, no. I kinda lied to you. But I was on deadline and had a spot to fill. You were the only guy that I could get on the phone."

"Well, why did he veto the funding?"

"Damn if I know. You need to ask Paul Wrotenberry, the state's Chief Budget Officer."

So, I went to Austin to ask Wrotenberry.

"Well, hell, Steve, it's a bullshit commission." Note the irony?

So I studied the Commission a bit, what they did, and they did do reasonably well. Wouldn't give them an A, but at least a B-.

One month later, I showed up at the first meeting to see what they planned to do. Reception and dinner the night before. I walked into reception quietly. Total silence, and the entire thirty-member commission turned to stare.

"Well, well, well, here comes the governor's appointee to tell us what he wants us to do."

Thirty sets of eyes staring at me.

A full fifteen seconds and no one spoke.

"Thank you, Mr. Chairman. Yes, I have been in touch with the governor's office. Let's relax and get to know each other over dinner. Tomorrow morning, I will share the plan with you."

That night, I prepared a plan. I was the only item on the agenda the next morning.

I presented my plan (never said it was the governor's plan, just that I had spoken with the governor's office). I planned to seek contracts from other government agencies to fund specific studies and add a 15 percent administrative fee. Not rocket science. They accepted that, and two years later, Governor Clements restored their funding.

Of significance to me, I was appointed to chair one of the studies: Model Rules for Law Enforcement, including the use of deadly force.

It was there that I learned the phrase "imminent risk of death or serious bodily injury." That knowledge would be of enormous use to me fifteen years later as mayor. More on that in the mayor's chapter.

In this case, **my purpose was leadership in public service** when the opportunity presented itself.

_AH HA!_ Be confident and have a plan.

The Byrd Rule

But that wasn't the end of the story. I went to all the meetings and participated. No heavy lift.

But six months into my service, I was surprised to be chosen as the Chairman of the Special Committee on Model Rules for Law Enforcement. These Model Rules were to be recommended to all law enforcement in Texas. Covered everything regarding police conduct and training to uniforms.

The big Kahuna of the report, of course, was the use of deadly force, i.e., "police shootings." And related subjects, such as when and how to make an arrest.

Don Byrd, then the Chief of Police of Dallas, was a member of the diverse thirty-member committee. In one session, the Committee got stuck on proper arrest techniques and when to handcuff. Some wanted more arrests, and some wanted fewer.

Don Byrd entered the fray with "The Byrd Rule," he said he taught new officers: "If you touch 'em, you'd better arrest 'em." Outrage was heard on all sides, of course. He then clarified with his corollary: "If you're not going to arrest them, don't touch them." We actually put that in the report.

A more inflammatory topic was the use of deadly force. Suspicions all around.

A young Assistant Attorney General wisely told me that to succeed, we would need the support of Hispanic leaders. He offered to introduce me to the legendary Dr. Hector P. Garcia, founder of the American GI Forum.

We drove to Corpus Christi to meet with Dr. Garcia. He was a bit surprised I would be asking his opinion. But he thanked me and said that if the report came out right, he would support it. And he did.

We started with the statutory standard, which is actually quite clear:

Deadly force may be used only with the risk of imminent death or major bodily injury.

All the excessive force controversies could be resolved by that standard. Any other use of deadly force was not only bad police practice, but illegal.

After hours of debate, the committee adopted the section on the use of deadly force unanimously.

Those words stuck with me when I became mayor. Chief Bill Rathburn, with my support, stopped the illegal police shootings cold.

My purpose was to improve police standards and slow the use of excessive force.

AH HA! When in doubt, follow the law.

CAMPAIGNING FOR CONGRESS

The Big Move: The U.S. Congress

Wick, Steve, and Jim: Three best friends.

In January 1981, Ronald Reagan took office and started the Reagan Revolution. Truly inspiring and exciting for me. The country was changing, and I wanted to be part of that change.

I enjoyed the city council, but it was clear to me and my close friends that if I wanted to change the country, I had to go where the laws were made: the U.S. Congress. The Federal budget, taxes, spending, and national security were all determined in Congress, so that's where I wanted to be.

A couple of immediate problems: First, so far as I knew, no one in Texas had gone directly from city council to the U.S. Congress in one step. Second, while I was reasonably popular in Dallas, most suburban voters had disdain for the Dallas City Council.

And since 1981 was a redistricting year, no one knew where the district lines would be. No problem. I drew a map of all the places in the district that might include my home: Plano to Mesquite, Highland Park to Garland, Farmers Branch to Lakewood. It was the size of two Congressional Districts. Divided it up by geography, identified the leaders (today called "influencers") in each area, and started introducing myself:

"In next year's Congressional election, there may be an open seat that includes your part of town. If so, I plan to run. I'm here to ask for your support. But more importantly, what do you think about the issues of the day?"

And for the first four months, I had it all to myself.

By the time the district lines were finalized, I had the foundation of a campaign in every part of the two districts. And better, the district where I lived was represented by Jim Mattox, who was quite disliked by most Republicans.

Assembled my informal Kitchen Cabinet: Jim, Wick, Enid, Rex, Mike. From June through August, we met every week or so, and I reported how it was going in each area.

I was ready, so I announced in the summer (that's very early), and Mattox withdrew two weeks later to run for Attorney General.

Primarily followed the "Campaign Coffee" Strategy: an informal event in a supporter's home, inviting both the supporter's friends *and other registered Republican voters in that precinct.* I introduced myself, shared why I wanted to be their congressman, and took questions.

Three messages: Effective. Conservative. Republican. Gail listened while knitting in the kitchen. And told me what I did wrong on the way home.

The brilliant Mike Lindley on the Kitchen Cabinet identified eight distinct areas and calculated exactly how many votes I needed from those areas to win overall. We planned the coffees to reach those areas proportionate to the target votes. By January of 1982, Gail and I had attended 175 coffees.

The secret sauce was to use my supporters' homes to meet voters I didn't know. My major opponent tended to meet only with his existing supporters.

I won't say it was masterful, but we basically had it won by late 1981.

Follow your purpose: get elected to Congress wherever the district lines are.

***AH HA!* Set your goals with clarity. Then implement with urgency.**

The Great Yard Sign War

Well, it wasn't actually a war. And the lesson wasn't really about yard signs.

Early in the campaign, in October 1981, my campaign manager, Jim DePetris, was contacted by a senior government class at Jesuit Dallas (a high school). Seems in their study of government, these seniors had figured out what most adults had not: most Congressional races are actually decided in the primary, most incumbents can't be beat and will serve at least ten years, and with redistricting in 1982, at least one open seat (no incumbent) would be available.

These seniors decided they could elect, or at least have a major influence in electing, someone to serve in the U.S. Congress for ten years.

They invited all known or rumored Congressional candidates in the area to be interviewed. There were eleven of us. Some didn't come. I'm told others were condescending.

I was impressed by these young adults, and told them so. Answered all their questions, and apparently made a good presentation. The class endorsed me and made my candidacy their class project.

They started with a five-man (Jesuit is an all-male school) Steering Committee headed by Dave Finn and Greg Ave. Recruited 100 volunteers from Jesuit and other area high schools (young men and women). That fall, they did a lot of the phone banks and mailings.

Then in February came the yard signs. These high schoolers built and distributed, in yards by permission, 5,000 yard signs. (My rule was no signs in public rights of way.)

Almost immediately, in the dead of night, most were torn down.

The Jesuit students were devastated and angry. They told DePetris they knew who did it and would not only "beat the hell out of them" but would also tear down all my opponents' signs.

Jim and I quickly conferred. We assembled our five leaders and established my expectations: we will not retaliate; I have purchased 5,000 more signs; we will build and re-distribute them next weekend. You are my leaders, and I expect you to lead and hold all others accountable.

They stepped up to the challenge. All signs were replaced, and no further yard signs were destroyed. In fact, in a couple of instances, supporters of one of my opponents called to say someone had stolen their signs. The Jesuit team delivered my opponents' signs to them.

These young adults learned a life lesson of responsibility and leadership. I kept up with several of them later in life, and several have told me this incident had a major effect on their lives.

I will always believe those young adults were a significant factor in my election.

A dual purpose: to get my 5,000 yard signs back up. **The bigger purpose was to build character in some young men.**

The icing on the cake was that ten years later, my son Brian attended and graduated from Jesuit, with a profound impact on his life.

AH HA! **It's not about yard signs. It's about accepting responsibility.**

Something Bad is About to Happen... No, Dad, It's Just the Birds

By end of 1981, I found myself way ahead. My major opponent in the 5th District was State Senator Dee Travis. He was a good candidate, but he basically talked to people who were already supporting him rather than reaching out to voters he didn't know.

By January 1982, I pretty much had it won, unless something unforeseen happened.

And something really, *really* unforeseen happened.

On a rainy Monday night in late January, I found myself mis-scheduled, which was a rarity. In fact, this had never happened. I showed up at 6:00 p.m. for a Men's Club at a big Episcopal Church. But I learned the Club was not until 7:30. Really big rainstorm, and the traffic was snarled, so I couldn't go to headquarters and get back in time.

I wandered around the church, into the chapel in the back. I sat down. May as well pray. A Voice came to me: *"It's about to get really bad. I mean really bad."*

"God is that you?"

"I'm telling you this so you'll be ready. You can handle it."

That's it. "What is it going to be?" I asked. "Cancer? A Traffic Accident? One of my kids gets sick?" The answer came a week later.

I went on about my business and worried about the Voice all week.

The following Saturday morning, I took my kids (Allison, Courtney, and Brian) on a camping trip to Possum Kingdom Lake. Our last weekend together before the door-to-door started. Turned off the radio so I didn't have to hear the news.

About 9:00 p.m. that night, around the campfire, Gail burst into the campfire circle. (Gail only camps on the 10th Floor of the Hilton Inn).

"I've driven to every camp around this lake and finally found you. You've got to go back now. The Federal Judge threw out your District and put you into the 3rd District with seven other candidates. Everyone in your campaign is panicking and needs you to tell them what to do."

Stunned, I gathered my thoughts. Too late to do anything about it tonight. And I promised the kids a camping trip. "Tell them I'll come back in the morning."

Secretly, I was relieved it was just politics rather than something serious like one of my kids getting sick.

The next morning at dawn, I took Brian, age four, to the lakeshore. Peaceful, serene. Just the sounds of the birds on the water.

"Brian, I'm sorry, but we have to go home a little early."

"Why, Dad?"

"Well, Brian, duty calls."

He cocked his head and listened, "Naw, Dad, it's just the birds."

I went back to Dallas, assembled the team, put together a new campaign plan, and ended up winning. And that was my purpose.

Jim Oberwetter later told me he had never seen me so calm.

My purpose was to stay calm and win the campaign,

AH HA!**When you think it's a disaster,
it's just the birds. And God.**

You're Free, I'll Tear Up the Contract

In assembling the team, I discovered most of my supporters in the 5th District had also been supporting other candidates in the 3rd District. I called together the Kitchen Cabinet, about fourteen key supporters, asked them to continue, but also said they were free to support another candidate.

After a grueling two-hour traumatic encounter, they all stayed with me.

One couple in particular stands out. Lisa Lemaster and her husband, Ken Fairchild, were professional media consultants. They had a contract with one of the other candidates, and it was far more lucrative than mine.

They told me the other candidate had told them they would sue to enforce the contract. So they had decided to drop out of both campaigns to avoid the conflict.

I replied that they shouldn't do that. I still wanted them, but I would tear up our contract and let them honor the other candidate to avoid getting them in trouble.

They stared at me for what seemed like three full minutes.

Finally, Lisa quietly said, "You don't have to do that. We'll tear up the other contract and let them sue."

This was retail politics at its most intense. A significant number of political allies had endorsed others in the 3rd and me in the 5th, so when we were thrown into the same district, it created great angst. I recall vividly one friend, a rising star in her mid-twenties named Jeanne Johnson, who later married and is known as Jeanne Johnson Phillips. I wanted her help.

So I invited her to lunch and asked her to join my campaign. She hemmed and hawed, but said she would stick with her original candidate. Truth is, I think she liked the other one more than she liked me.

"I understand. I respect that, and I hope we can still be friends.

"But if I win the nomination, remember there is a place for you in my campaign."

Jeanne arrived at my Victory Party after the results were known. To volunteer to help. No hard feelings.

Jeanne became one of my best friends and most ardent supporters. She was the finance director in my mayoral campaign, among other things, and a permanent member of the famed Lunch Bunch.

Of course, she also became George W. Bush's finance director as governor and as president. She went on to be GWB's ambassador to the OECD in Paris and introduced my daughter, Courtney, to her future husband.

The purpose was to invite and welcome support, not force it.

Sure glad I was nice to her at lunch.

AH HA! **You can't buy loyalty. Be nice to everyone.**

Turn On the Sprinklers and Let Out the Dogs, But Never Miss a Cowboys Game

Altogether, Gail and I did 515 "Campaign Coffees" in the 3rd and the 5th Districts from June 1981 to November 1982. These don't really serve coffee; it's just an expression, so people wouldn't think it was a fundraiser. Always in a supporter's home who furnished the refreshments. Size ranged from two in Rowlett (that was awkward) to 200+ on Swiss Avenue. We typically invited all the Republican voters in the precinct, and depended on the host to invite friends.

Gail and I always went together. During the busiest times, we could do three in one evening: 6:00, 7:30, 8:30. Just as in the early days, Gail always sat watching from the kitchen, knitting, so she could tell me what I did wrong on the way home. She pulled no punches.

Did I mention Gail is a saint? While attending three coffees every night, she also had a full-time job helping support the family and keeping track of our three children. We did have a live-in "nanny" named Kari who watched the kids at night in exchange for room and board. Kari became Gail's best friend and is to this day.

All the coffees were memorable, but one of the most unusual was in a mobile home park in Pleasant Grove. I was excited about this one because mobile home parks are hard to get into, a lot of suspicion, and not many Republicans.

It was dark when we arrived. Chain link fence. As we got to the gate, the owner called out loudly, "Get out!" Followed by letting out a big snarling dog and turning on the water sprinkler.

We ran back to the car before "Cujo" could get us. Shaking off the water and out of breath.

"Well, Sweetheart, I guess we'll just mark that one Undecided!"

We both laughed and drove to the next coffee.

On the other end of the spectrum, a friend, Robert, on Swiss Avenue (large stately mansions) held a coffee on a Sunday afternoon at a time that conflicted with a televised Cowboys game. When I expressed concern about the conflict, he was a bit offended, "My friends *do not* watch football on TV," he sniffed.

Sure enough, over 200 of Dallas' finest arrived, some in limos. It was a record turnout.

Before my speech, I went up the spiral staircase to gather my thoughts and use the facilities. Right there, in the upstairs parlor, watching the Cowboys game, was Robert's mother by herself. She told me the score and who caught the touchdown pass.

I kept her secret from her son, Robert.

My purpose was to win votes in every part of the District.

_AH HA!_ Whatever the question,
coffee is the answer.

God Does Indeed Work in Mysterious Ways

I almost did not include this. It's personal and spiritual, not political.

In September 1981, my campaign was functioning, but not fully staffed. We were raising money with a combination of mailings to supporters and a finance committee chaired by the awesome Bill Schilling, Managing Partner of KPMG.

Doing well, but not hitting on all cylinders. One of the volunteers from the Young Republican Club, Sylvia, offered to serve as volunteer finance director. She had no campaign experience, but she was bright, energetic, and had leadership skills.

By November, it was clear we needed some professional help, but we couldn't afford it.

The Republican National Committee announced a fundraising training school. I asked Sylvia to attend at our expense. She agreed, but asked if she could bring her friend, Mary, and pay her airfare.

Of course, I said yes.

Sylvia and Mary came back and helped to organize our fundraising efforts.

Sylvia then confided that the real reason Mary wanted to go to Washington was that she had just heard from her father for the first time in twenty years. He had recently contacted her from Washington, D.C., where he was living. He wanted to reconnect. She had not seen or heard from him since she was four years old.

She met with him twice while in Washington, and they had a tearful and meaningful reconciliation.

Then came American Airlines Flight 90 on January 13, 1982, crashing into the Potomac, killing seventy-eight passengers.

Sylvia called to tell me that Mary's father was on that plane, and in fact, she thinks he was the unidentified man who went back into the Potomac to rescue passengers. He died while attempting the rescue.

Mary profoundly believes that this was not a coincidence, but **God's purpose was for Mary and her father to meet before he died.**

As do I.

AH HA! **We don't know God's Plan, but He does. And we can often see the results.**

The Last Debate: Stay on Message

The last debate of round one came on a Wednesday for the Saturday election. All seven candidates lined up to get their last shots in.

Sam Attelsey, Chief Political Reporter of the Dallas News, claimed the last question.

"Candidates, last question: Is there any issue on which you have been treated unfairly by the media? Here's your chance to set the record straight."

No meaningful answers except my leading opponent launched a strident attack on me by name. Claiming, "the press has never, *never* reported Steve Bartlett's real position on abortion. He is rigidly pro-life, and it has never been reported." Pointing a finger at me: "Mr. Bartlett, I demand you reveal your real position on abortion."

(*Side note:* I am pro-life, and that *had* been reported. But I didn't campaign on it. My issues were all economic.)

I stared straight ahead to gather my thoughts. How should I respond? Once again, Jim Oberwetter to the rescue. He caught my eye from the back of the room.

And with a subtle shake of his head, he reminded me. "Stay on message."

"Sam, you asked if there was anything I wished the press had covered differently. Yes, there is one thing. I wish the press had reported more about the federal deficit and its negative effect on the economy. That's what's important."

My purpose was to win the election, not just the debate.

Check. Checkmate.

***AH HA!* Stay on message.**

Just Be Nice: Split Screen Surprise

Courtney on the left and Allison on the right with their dad on congressional election night

Round one was seven candidates, and then a five-week runoff. I was constantly aware that when runoff time came, I would have to appeal to the voters who had voted for my opponents. Meaning, I never said an unkind word about any of my opponents.

On many days, the candidates would be in the same place at least once. So I made it a point to chat amiably with each one: ask about family, commiserate about how grueling the campaign was, and so forth. Knowing I needed their endorsement for the runoff.

Little did I know my playing nice would work out so well.

By 9:00 p.m. on election night, it was clear Kay and I would face each other in a runoff. She was actually ahead.

Channel 8 sent a TV crew to three victory parties: First Place Kay Hutchison, Third Place Jim Jackson, and me in second place. Three-way split screen. Live. Drama.

After the initial statements, the reporter asked Jim Jackson, "Do you plan to endorse in the runoff? And if so, when?" Not really expecting an answer.

Jackson, without hesitation, "I know who I'm going to endorse, and I'll endorse him right now: Steve Bartlett."

Live TV. Jackson looking resolute, straight into the camera. Me, with a nice smile, saying on live TV, "Thank you, Jim. I wasn't expecting that, but I do appreciate it."

That was on a Saturday night. The next morning, my campaign decided that I should take being nice one step further: *Be nice to everyone.* So I recorded a radio spot for Monday morning drive time. Thanking the voters for their confidence in me. No issues, just a thank you.

And I had the momentum. The runoff was on.

The purpose, in all these stories, was to win the election, to accomplish the greater good in Congress.

AH HA! Be nice to everyone. All the time

Tell Them Who You are, and Keep it Positive

There were lots of issues. Back and forth. But mostly, the campaign was Republican voters trying to size up who could best represent them in Congress. Early on, I would sit in the kitchen of Republican precinct leaders as they would "examine" me, peppering all manner of, "What would you do if this or that happened? Who are your heroes? What are you most afraid of?"

I recall one conversation, quite well, that did not go my way. A prominent leader of the largest Republican Women's Club came to my headquarters early on to demand, "Steve, I'm looking for a congressman who will not think about issues too much. Just vote like Jesse Helms and don't try to think about it."

Gulp. "Well, I understand what you're saying. If you want a rubber stamp for Jesse Helms, then I'm not your guy. I'm going to think about every vote, and vote the way I think is best for the country. Every time. You should not vote for me." I did not add that Jesse Helms was definitely not my hero.

My last mailer in round one summed it up. It was Friday night, and we had time and money for one more mailer. Media Consultant Enid Gray, best friends Wick Allison and Jim Oberwetter, and I were stuck on what it should say. Batted around ideas for a couple of hours. Nothing.

Visibly frustrated and a little angry, I stood up. "I have a coffee to attend. You three sit here all night if you have to, but don't leave until you get it right!" I stormed out.

Shocked and a little irritated at my intemperance, Wick said, "You know, Tip O'Neill is going to hate that guy."

What? That was it. That was the last mailer: "Tip O'Neill will hate Steve Bartlett" on the outside of the envelope. Inside the envelope, you learned why the Democratic Speaker would hate Republican Steve Bartlett. Not personal, just on the issues.

Our phones rang off the wall. "Why is Tip O'Neill attacking Steve Bartlett?" "Please open the envelope, and you will see why." Some Republicans were so mad that they refused to open it, so a volunteer had to read it to them.

You might say I ran against Tip. I don't think he ever knew.

In this case, the purpose was simply to get them to open the envelope.

_AH HA!_ When in doubt, show them what you're against.

Why is the National Rifle Association Mad?

Lisa Stoltenberg had been a friend and political ally since the Tom Pauken for State Senate campaign in 1976. She moved to Washington, D.C., and was active in Republican politics. She went on to work for me in Congress and later at the Roundtable.

She knew that most of the Washington Republican groups were staying out of the primary, waiting to support the Republican nominee. Some were supporting me (homebuilders and realtors, energy PACs, and Frito-Lay, I recall), but most were neutral.

About midway through the runoff, Lisa had a brainstorm. She called my campaign manager, Jim DePetris, and asked him to go to Austin and look for gun control votes in the Legislature. He sent young activist Mike Solon, who spent all night reading legislative votes from three sessions.

Bingo! (Or bull's-eye.) Kay had voted to ban the sale of Chinese-made .38 handguns. Her husband, Ray, and Fred Agnich, the father of Kay's campaign chairman, and most Republicans had voted no. Actually, so had most Democrats.

Lisa called the NRA and showed them the voting record. Within days, the NRA telephoned its 5,000 members in the 3rd District. Five thousand!

In fairness, I had answered "undecided" on a three-day waiting period for firearm purchases. The NRA told Lisa this, but Kay's vote gave them cause to endorse me.

Kay was outraged and said so very publicly for several days. My only response was, "I don't know why the NRA is so mad at Kay. You'll have to ask them."

The story lingered for a week.

My purpose was to communicate with voters.

AH HA! Never get in a fight with 5,000 members.

He's a Liar!

Things went back and forth.

Then disaster hit, or near disaster.

The smallest part of my district was Garland. Garland had been carved up in the Federal Court Redistricting and lost its prominence. Garland had its own daily newspaper. I had told the editor much earlier that the reason Garland got screwed over was that the State Republican Party had refused to appeal the redistricting court order.

That was true, but a big mistake on my part. *Big mistake. Big Mistake!* Don't go out looking for enemies. Two weeks before election day, the editor called the State GOP Chairman, Chet Upham, and asked him about that.

Not only did he deny it, but he was incensed that I would say such a thing. Then his words made banner headlines in the Garland Daily News. *"STEVE BARTLETT IS A LIAR!"*

Fortunately, it happened on a Friday. On Saturday morning, I went to our regular Kitchen Cabinet.

I was furious. "I am not a liar, and I can prove it. Phone records, letters, witnesses, court documents. Get the press in here, and I will prove I'm not a liar." They stared at me.

Jim Oberwetter again saved the day. "Steve, sit down and don't say another word." Jim had run into the iconic GOP leader Peter O'Donnell in the elevator at work and asked him what to do.

As he stepped off the elevator, Peter simply said, "Change the subject."

It was obvious to Jim and the others that my approach would be a bigger disaster than the first headline. "He's a liar." "I am not." "Yes, he is." And all the voters would hear was "Steve Bartlett Liar."

So Jim and Enid concocted the plan: change the subject.

On Sunday afternoon, we released a poll showing I was supported by 67.2 percent of the Republican Precinct Chairmen. A small sample, but it was 67.2 percent.

For the next four days, we debated who was ahead. And "Liar" was not mentioned again. Whew.

Once again, **Jim Oberwetter reminded me of my purpose.**

AH HA! **When you're losing the argument, change the subject.**

Nobody's Going to Believe That

And one more big shock that rocked my world, but turned out to matter not at all.

Background: Six months before redistricting changed everything, Jim and I were hanging out at Joe Miller's bar one night. Joe Miller's bar was where politicians and reporters could mingle and talk off the record.

At the time, I was campaigning feverishly in the 5th District, and Kay in the 3rd. Ray Hutchison (Kay's husband), Jim, myself, and the aforementioned Sam Attlesey were enjoying a few rounds at the end of the day.

Ray then pulled some handwritten letters out of his pocket. "Look at this, Sam." They were vile, disgusting, anonymous letters, attacking Kay and Ray viciously. Sam said, "Can I run the story?" "No, it's off the record," Ray replied, putting the letters back in his pocket.

Fast forward eight months to the 3rd District runoff. Wednesday before the Saturday runoff. Last coffee. Lisa LeMaster, my amazing media director, came to get me. "Sam Attlesey is on the phone. He's on deadline. Asking about the letters."

Huh? What letters?

"Sam, what's this about? "

You know, Ray showed you those letters six months before I was even in the race."

"Yep, but that was off the record."

"Now we are on the record. Ray is accusing you of writing those letters."

In fairness to Sam, I realize he had to report the accusation and my response. Not fair, but Journalism 101.

"I'm running the story."

In shock, I stumbled back to the coffee. The first guy I saw was Adolf Hauntz, a big, affable butcher from South Dallas. He said I looked like I had seen a ghost.

I told him about the story that would run in Thursday's paper

Adolf laughed. A big, deep belly laugh (and Adolf had quite a belly).

"How can you laugh? This could defeat me with one untrue newspaper story."

Then Adolf got serious. "Steve, people know you. Nobody's going to believe that about you. Get a good night's sleep."

Adolf was right. The story ran, and not a single person ever asked me about it. Not one.

My purpose was to be true to myself.

***AH HA!* If people know you, they will not believe a lie.**

It's Still Not Over Until the Last Vote is Counted

Gail and Steve on election primary night. June 1982

Remember my city council story about "don't predict your win until you win"? This is similar.

Runoff Election Day 1982. I spent the day visiting the six phone banks we had around the District, thanking the several hundred volunteers calling to remind people to vote.

My last stop was our main headquarters. Polls closed at 7:00 p.m.. At 6:40 p.m., one of the volunteers shouted, "I've got Mrs. Smith, who needs a ride to the polls. She lives on Caruth Street. Does anyone know where Caruth is?"

Several minutes of a mad scramble looking for a MAPSCO. No such luck.

Now it's 6:45. I shout, "Give me the address, I know where Caruth is."

As I am running out the door, the volunteer shouts, "Steve, Mrs. Smith is blind."

I arrive at Mrs. Smith's door at 6:52. She is ready for me.

"Mrs. Smith, I'm Steve Bartlett. I'm here to take you to vote."

A cross look came over her face. "Don't you go fooling an old blind lady. I want to vote for Steve Bartlett. You're not Steve Bartlett."

"Mrs. Smith, we don't have much time. I'll explain in the car."

Mrs. Smith cast her vote at 6:57 p.m.

If I had won by one vote…

A noble purpose is to count every vote.

***AH HA!* Don't stop until the last vote is counted.**

Congressman, We Saw You at the Bar Last Night

I had one more lesson to learn. The hard way. Gail and I, along with my circle of friends, had been campaigning intensely for a year and a half. Every day was in the spotlight, and every word and mannerism was scrutinized.

I decided to get out of town and relax, to let my hair down. So Gail and I, Jim, Wick, Ken and Lisa, Jim DePetris, and a few others booked a three-day weekend on South Padre Island, 580 miles from Dallas. We could let our hair down because no one would know us.

Wrong.

Saturday night at South Padre Island. I was invisible, or so I thought, and I let my hair down. Gail kept telling me to stop drinking, but I told her it was safe because we weren't in Dallas and these were friends. I got blitzed.

The next day, at the Harlingen airport returning to Dallas, a couple approached me with a funny look. "Congressman, we're from Dallas, and we saw you at the bar last night. Boy, you were sure having a good time."

Whoops. I learned then, and I've never forgotten it. When you are a public official, you are never off duty, never invisible.

My purpose should have been not to embarrass myself.

AH HA! You're never off duty.

THE U.S. CONGRESS: THE HEART OF THE REAGAN REVOLUTION

Get There Early and Stay Late

Steve arriving in Washington with his family (January 1983) as a newly elected congressman

Since my primary victory was in June, and the general election was in November, I had more time than most to prepare. I knew what issues most interested me, and I knew my general purpose was "to pass good legislation and defeat bad legislation." But I didn't know exactly how.

I decided to ask those who did know. I made several trips to Washington. Relying on the "80/20 Rule," which means that in every organization, 20 percent of the members do 80 percent of the work.

So I started asking around Capitol Hill, "Who is the 20 percent who really run this place? Who gets things done? How can I succeed?"

I then made a list and interviewed 100 members of Congress, from both groups. One question: What should a young freshman do to succeed?

I classified the answers into two groups:

- Group One, the 80 percent: Don't even try. Just get your newsletters out and get re-elected. Then, when you've been here ten years or more, you'll have the seniority to accomplish something.

- Group Two, the 20 percent: You can do anything you set out to do, starting on your first day. Just follow a few simple concepts.

Following is my summary of those simple rules from Group Two, the "You can do anything you set out to do": Get there early and stay late.

1. Do your homework; know more about the subject than anyone else in the room.

2. Follow the rules, including the rules of civility and courtesy.

3. And never, ever, *ever* give up.

Know the rules. I hired Pete Madigan, a former Floor Assistant to Leadership, for a ninety-day assignment to teach me the rules, written and unwritten. That was his only job, and he did it very well.

Those who told me "Do your homework, follow the rules, get there early, and stay late" were the ones running the place.

I printed these concepts and gave each staff member a copy upon hire.

I set my purpose early: pass good legislation and defeat bad legislation.

_AH HA!_ Get there early and stay late. You can accomplish anything.

It all Starts With Committee Assignments

In the House of Representatives, unlike the Senate, every member of Congress is expected to specialize in the areas under their committee's jurisdiction. You can have an opinion on everything, but your opinion only carries weight on matters within your committee's jurisdiction.

Sad and frustrating, but my survey of senior members confirmed this truth.

Committee assignments are made by the secretive "Committee on Committees." I knew who was on the Committee, but had no way of knowing what was said in their deliberations. I did meet with every member of the Committee, but so did every other freshman.

In short, things did not go well. Not sure why, but looking back, I think I was regarded as too brash, and maybe arrogant. I was assigned to two meaningless committees: the Joint Economic Committee and Oversight. Neither had legislative jurisdiction.

And my mantra for being in Congress was to pass good legislation and defeat bad legislation.

I went to one of my mentors, Tom Loeffler of Texas, Chief Deputy Whip.

He wanted to help. On the day of the vote for committee assignments, he walked me to Bob Michel, House Republican Leader.

"Bob's response was less than inspiring. "Golly gee whiz, I don't know what I can do. The Committee on Committees has voted. But I will go to Tom Foley, the Democratic Leader. and ask. Wait here."

And then, lightning struck. When Bob went to Tom, it seemed Tom Foley had his own problem. Phil Burton, powerful Chairman of the House Rules Committee, had promised a seat on the sought-after Banking and Urban Affairs (i.e., housing) Committee to Esteban Torres. But he had forgotten his promise until that very afternoon.

Bob came back with a smile. "Foley has agreed to add two seats to Banking, and you can have the Republican seat."

Tom Loeffler, thinking quickly, said, "Bob, in exchange for the seat on Banking, Bartlett will accept a seat on the unpopular Education and Labor Committee. He will be your only conservative."

In the space of ten minutes, I had gone from no legislative priorities to five: Banking, Housing, Education, Labor, and Disability.

Bob literally penciled my name onto the bottom of the list as we walked to the House Floor. And my legislative career was launched. I became an activist and leader on all five.

My purpose was focused: to obtain committee assignments to pass good legislation.

And with those committee assignments, I wrote and passed eighteen bills that became law.

You can't make this stuff up.

_AH HA!_ Pass good legislation and defeat bad.

The Smallest Subcommittee

One thing I learned in these interviews was the power of committee staff. Committee staff, also known as "professional staff," write the legislation.

But how do you get committee staff?

I had always been interested in disability issues. It turned out that the Education and Labor Committee had a subcommittee called the Select Education Subcommittee. It was one of the smallest subcommittee in Congress. All the issues few cared about, including disability, were assigned to this subcommittee.

And it had one staff member.

I went to my GOP Committee Caucus with a plan. I was the last to choose a subcommittee. I said, "Select Education." Since I was the first to choose that subcommittee, that made me the ranking member, who hires the staff.

The other congressmen tried to talk me out of it. "It's too hard, you're too new, the issues are too raw."

I held my ground, politely.

I returned to my office. The phone rang. It was John Erlenborn, Ranking Member of the full committee. He had figured out my game.

"Mr. Bartlett, you know Select Education has committee staff. And in *ordinary circumstances,* the ranking member of the subcommittee chooses the staff."

Yes, I did know that.

"So to be clear, you can hire any staff you choose, so long as her name is Dr. Patricia Morrissey. I hired her myself four years ago, and I am very loyal to her."

"Yes, Mr. Erlenborn. In fact, Pat Morrissey is exactly who I plan to hire."

He smiled over the phone. "I'm glad we understand each other."

Pat Morrissey stayed with me for my entire career and was largely responsible for passing five major pieces of disability legislation, including the Americans with Disabilities Act, my signature accomplishment.

My purpose was to hire good staff, even if they were sent by someone else.

AH HA! **Nothing happens without staff.**

Mr. Burton Died. Go to the Beach

April 1983. Gail and I had been in this congressional thing since June 1981. A grueling primary campaign, then a long general election campaign, then the transition: selling the house, moving the family, buying a new house, driving to Washington, hiring staff, and getting up to speed on my seven committee and subcommittee assignments. All while trying to figure out how to get home before the kids' bedtime and still have time for Gail.

Needless to say, Gail and I were at the end of our rope.

Then, in early April, my main mentor and Republican Whip, Trent Lott, approached me on the House floor.

"Steve, Mr. Burton died." Phil Burton was the feared chairman of the House Rules Committee.

"Okay," I said, curious. "What does that have to do with me?"

"This place is going to shut down next week, all week, for the funeral in San Francisco. Over half the House will attend.

"But you are new, and you didn't know Mr. Burton, so you don't have to go. Instead, go back to your office right now, I mean <u>now,</u> call Gail and your travel agent, hire a babysitter, and book a four-day holiday on the beach with your wife."

"Why?" I asked. "Shouldn't I go home to work in the district?"

"Because you've been burning both ends of the candle, and you look like hell. I bet Gail does too. This is your last chance to get your head on straight."

We spent four glorious days in the Virgin Islands, on the beach, and it was the best decision I made that year.

I never met Phil Burton, but Gail and I still remember him fondly.

In this case, my purpose was to strengthen my marriage.

AH HA! **Take care of home business first, and go to the beach.**

Pay Your Own Damn Traffic Ticket

In the summer of 1983, I drove to downtown D.C. to make a speech to a business group. I parked at a meter, stayed too long, and came back to find a parking ticket.

I had U.S. Congress license plates and had been told by the Sergeant at Arms that I could park anywhere I wanted with those "Official Business" plates.

The next day, enraged, I found another mentor of mine, Bill Frenzel of Minnesota. He had been in Congress for twenty years and was very level-headed.

"Bill, look at this! I had U.S. Congress plates, I was on official business, and furthermore, the U.S. Constitution protects congressmen from arrest while on official business.

"Should I take this to the Sergeant at Arms and have him fix the ticket?"

"Well, you can do that, and he will fix the ticket. And you would read about it in the *Dallas Morning News* by the weekend. So is that worth a $25 parking ticket?"

Oh. I understood. Thank you, wise Bill Frenzel. I paid the ticket.

My purpose was to do the right thing, even if I didn't have to.

_AH HA!_ You ain't so special,
pay your own damn ticket.

New York Gets Half, the Rest of You Get the Other Half

A feature of American culture in the twentieth and twenty-first centuries is the so-called "Flyover States." That is, the snobbish tendency of the Northeast and the West Coast is ever-present.

The Select Education Subcommittee had jurisdiction over the National Endowment for the Arts (NEA) as well as disability issues, my primary interest. My committee chairman, Pat Williams of Montana, was very interested in the NEA and not so much in disability. So, if I helped him on the NEA, he would allow me to do my work on disability.

Pat wanted to have a hearing in New York on the arts. He needed me to attend as a Republican, or he couldn't hold the hearing. I agreed, of course.

The first witness was Bess Myerson, former Miss America and commissioner of the arts for New York City. She began enthusiastically extolling the many good things the endowment had done in New York City.

Five minutes in, she stopped and looked at our nameplates:
"Williams – Montana." "Bartlett – Texas." Oops.

She stammered and stared. After a long silence, she said, "Mr. Williams, Mr. Bartlett, the National Endowment serves the whole country, not just New York City. In fact, only half of NEA funds go to New York City. The other half goes to the rest of the country. I mean, that's fair, isn't it? I mean, half for us and half for everyone else?"

She stared. Pat and I didn't know what to say. After all, this was Miss America.

Finally, Pat leaned over, smiled, and said, "Why don't you just proceed with your testimony, Miss Myerson?"

And the final bill, while not perfect, created a slightly more even distribution of funding.

My purpose was not to score cheap political points but to write a good bill.

AH HA! **It's a big country.**

Hello Brian, Where's Your Dad?

Brian meets President Reagan in 1983

During my first term, the Bartlett family was invited to the Oval Office to meet the president for the classic photo op. President Reagan was warm and gracious, visiting with each of my children individually and paying special attention to Gail. It earned me some extra brownie points at home, and the photo went on the family Christmas card.

The whole visit took fifteen minutes at most, and I figured the president would not remember it fifteen minutes later.

Boy, did I underestimate Ronald Reagan.

The next day was the Congressional Family Picnic on the South Lawn. In fact, that's why we had been invited to the Oval Office, as Gail was one of the organizers of the picnic.

Gail was busy doing her thing and assigned six-year-old Brian to me, admonishing, "Don't let him get in trouble."

Brian and I got our BBQ plates and headed to the back of the lawn, thinking we could stay out of the way.

Bad call. The back was actually the front, where the VIPs sat.

Here came President and Mrs. Reagan and all the congressional leadership. They sat down one table away.

Before I could collect my wits, Brian jumped up and ran to the president's table, tapped him on the shoulder, and as Ronald Reagan turned around, Brian announced, "Hi, remember me?"

"Why yes, Brian, I enjoyed meeting you yesterday. Where's your dad?"

"Over there," Brian said, pointing.

The president looked over at me, waved, and smiled. He may have said something like, "I'll send him back."

Don't ever let anyone say otherwise. Ronald Reagan was on top of things.

Ronald Reagan's purpose on this day was to be kind to a six-year-old.

AH HA! **Presidents are people too. And hold on to your six-year-old.**

Mr. Bartlett, You Do Nice Work

Remember my mantra: "Do your homework. Follow the rules, including civility and courtesy."

From my experience in Dallas, I knew something about the disastrous state of disrepair in public housing. It was a true national scandal.

I learned that the proposed appropriation for public housing included five billion dollars for new construction and almost nothing for repair. I offered a floor amendment to take half the new construction funds and send them to repair and modernization.

The barriers seemed insurmountable. I was a freshman, only seven months in office, not on the Appropriations Committee, and I was taking money away from new projects that had already been "promised."

Then I was told the real problem: the chairman of the subcommittee was Ed Boland of Massachusetts—*the Eddie Boland.* A congressman for twenty-five years, revered by all. Cary Grant central casting looks. He had federal laws named after him and had singlehandedly changed American foreign policy in Nicaragua with "The Boland Amendment."

He had never been bested in a floor fight. Never.

Experts told me not to try. "He will embarrass you," they said.

I lined up support from both Democrats and Republicans. I did my homework. I had the facts. I was respectful and courteous. The debate lasted six hours. It grew somewhat vicious from others, but not from Mr. Boland or me.

I won on a close roll call. After the vote, when most others had left the floor, Mr. Boland walked to the Republican side, held out his hand, and said, "Mr. Bartlett, you do nice work."

My purpose was to literally improve the living conditions of tens of thousands of public housing residents.

***AH HA!* Courtesy and civility go a long way.**

I'm Going to Cut His Balls Off

The perfect contrast to Ed Boland was Jack Brooks from Beaumont, Texas. He was chairman of the powerful Government Operations Committee and was known for punishing his adversaries severely. He was often called "The Meanest Man in Congress."

During my first recess, I was told by Jake Pickle, a powerful but kind Democratic congressman from Austin, that I had parked in Jack Brooks's parking space at National Airport.

"Wait, there are no assigned parking spaces at National."

"Except for Mr. Brooks's parking space, even though his name is not on it. You're expected to know. And you should go to Mr. Brooks and apologize." I did.

During my second term, an appropriations bill came to the floor that included various pork-barrel special projects. One such project was for a constituent, friend, and supporter of Jack Brooks. Disgusting? Yes. About $100 million or so.

Jim Kolbe, a freshman congressman from Arizona, was incensed and offered an amendment to remove the Jack Brooks project. I was watching from the back rail when Jack came to the House floor with fire in his eyes. He quickly found me.

"Bartlett, you know this fella Kolbe?"

"Yes, I do."

"I'm gonna cut his balls off."

Uh oh. That meant Jack would order an IRS or DOJ investigation on Kolbe, or worse.

"Mr. Brooks, let me tell you two things. First, Kolbe is a pretty good guy, and if you let him survive, he will make a pretty good congressman. Second, this amendment will fail. I guarantee it. Now, don't be surprised, I'm going to vote for it, but it will fail because most congressmen are not going to cross you."

"You guarantee it will fail?"

"Yep. I guarantee it."

"Okay, I won't cut his balls off." And he stormed off.

The amendment failed. Brooks's supporter did not get the money, and Kolbe went on to serve a distinguished career of almost thirty years.

Purpose: save Kolbe's political career.

***AH HA!* All's well that ends well.**

Two Hours in the Senate Cloak Room

Late in my first term as a freshman congressman. In fact, it was the last day of the 1984 session.

As ranking Republican for the Select Education Subcommittee, I led the legislation to reauthorize the $1 billion Vocational Rehabilitation Act. It was a twenty-month effort, and we made significant improvements.

The bill was stuck in the Senate, and we were scheduled to adjourn at midnight. At 5:00 p.m., Senator Orrin Hatch called me.

"Steve, we've run into a little snag. Can you come over to the Senate Republican Cloakroom, and we can work it out?"

"May I bring my Chairman?"

"Of course."

The chairman was the iconic Democrat Carl Perkins of Kentucky, a true gentleman and a firm believer in government programs. He had served in Congress since 1948 and had chaired the Education and Labor Committee since sometime in the 1960s.

We arrived in the Senate Republican Cloakroom. Orrin brought Lowell Weicker, the liberal GOP firebrand from Connecticut. He was "the snag."

It seemed Lowell had a last-minute demand that we add a new "Office of Legal Counsel" to the bill. Reading the details, this office would have the authority to sue state agencies. It was a truly radical idea, but Orrin was inclined to accept it as a favor to a fellow Republican.

I said absolutely not. No hearings, no record, last-minute, and big trouble for the states.

Lowell held firm. In fact, he became quite animated, yelling and threatening. Twice, the Senate sergeant at arms came into the cloakroom to tell me to keep my voice down. (I wasn't yelling; Lowell was. But he wasn't going to tell a senator to hush.)

After two hours, Orrin agreed to strike the provision. Lowell stormed out.

Mr. Perkins and I walked slowly back to the House Floor to pass the bill.

Mr. Perkins, who hadn't said more than six words, put his arm over my shoulders and said, "Mr. Bartlett, you do nice work."

That was the second time that session I had heard those words.

Once again, **the purpose was to pass good legislation.**

AH HA! **Keep your cool and don't back down.**

Dave, Come See Me At About 3:00 p.m.

Briefing the president in the Roosevelt Room, 1984

Beginning about 1978, one of the major movements in the United States was known as "Education Reform." End social promotion. No Pass, No Play. Twenty years later, it became "No Child Left Behind."

By late 1983, education reform had finally arrived in Washington, led by a commission report prepared by the Department of Education entitled *A Nation at Risk: The Imperative for Educational Reform.*

I joined a new Education Reform Caucus of Republicans to advance the cause. The only problem was that no one had told President Reagan.

In the spring of 1984, I learned through back-channel sources that OMB Director Dave Stockman intended to "zero out" the entire Department of Education in the upcoming proposed budget. It would never happen, of course, but the damage would be that congressional Republicans would have no credibility on education reform.

I rounded up the members of our caucus, John Erlenborn, Bill Goodling, Vin Weber, and Mickey Edwards, and we asked for a meeting with the president.

In the Roosevelt Room, we were seated around the elegant table. Vice President George Bush, Dave Stockman, Ed Meese, Jim Baker, and Secretary of Education Terrell Bell were there.

The president came in. You could almost hear "Hail to the Chief."

"Gentlemen, I understand you wanted to talk about education." He then read from his speech cards the standard stump speech he had been delivering for twenty years: "Abolish the Department of Education and put prayer back in schools. Now, what's on your mind?"

Gulp.

Because I had asked for the meeting, I went first (and maybe they were throwing me under the bus). I laid out the case for education reform and showed him the report, giving a few highlights. The White House photographer captured the scene with me leaning across the table, pointing at Ronald Reagan. It is my favorite photo on the wall.

Nobody moved. It was clear that the president knew none of this.

He turned to Secretary Bell. "Is this true, Terrell?"

"Well, uh, er, I mean, well, yes."

We went around the table, and my GOP colleagues backed me up.

The president said not a word, but he was clearly intrigued by the new information. He turned to Mickey Edwards, Oklahoma congressman and, more importantly, president of the National Conservative Union.

"What do you think, Mickey?"

Pointing at me, Mickey just said, "The kid's right."

President Reagan stood and thanked us for coming. As he reached the door, he turned to Dave Stockman.

"Dave, can you come see me at about three o'clock?"

The president left. Not a word was spoken until Stockman turned to me and said, "You won, you son of a bitch."

And education reform became a Republican issue. That was my purpose.

AH HA! Don't forget to brief the president.

George W. Bush: Baseball or Governor?

This kind of falls into the category of "kiss and tell," but it is not unfavorable, so I will tell it.

In 1990 there was a hot Democratic primary for governor of Texas, and the Republicans had not settled on a candidate. George W. Bush, the vice president's son, was in the oil business in Dallas. Several of the big-dog Republican leaders tried to recruit George W., but he wouldn't hear of it.

As the local Republican congressman, I was called on to talk him into it.

We met at Kel's, the local crowded and noisy "greasy spoon" I favored for breakfast, a good-old-boy hangout. I made my ask and reminded him who had sent me.

George leaned over and lowered his voice, looking around to make sure no one could hear.

"Steve, everything you say is true. I could run, probably win, and make a decent governor. But here's the problem: I have a chance to buy a major-league baseball team."

"What would you choose, baseball or governor?"

"Well, hell, George, baseball, of course. Anybody can be governor, but few can own a baseball team."

"That's what I thought, Steve. Now don't you tell those sons of bitches. They'd buy it out from under me."

He bought the team and became governor four years later.

He accomplished both purposes.

AH HA! **When in doubt, choose baseball.**

FHA: Someone Changed the Law

A housing bill signing ceremony

If I ever had any doubt about whether what I did mattered in real people's lives, that doubt was put to rest in late 1984.

I had offered another really controversial amendment in early 1983 that would allow the FHA interest rate to be set by the market rather than regulated by the Secretary of HUD, as had been the case for forty years.

It might sound like a small thing, but a system of setting interest rates by administrative fiat is always flawed. Set it too high and buyers get priced out. Set it too low and sellers pull their property off the market rather than pay the difference.

It was a massive floor fight that lasted eight hours and took two roll call votes. Harsh words were said by many. Subcommittee Chairman Henry

Gonzales even took out hour-long "Special Orders" two or three times a week to condemn me by name.

My amendment became law.

While I thought it was a big deal, my role didn't even make the Dallas papers. I didn't think much more about it until eighteen months later. I was a speaker at a Dallas civic club dinner. Making small talk with the wife of the club president, I asked, "What's new in your life?"

"I'm so glad you asked. I am so excited. We just bought our first house last week. We tried to buy a house two years ago. Had an FHA loan. Got to closing and everything blew up. We lost the house. Something about points and the market changed.

"I thought we'd never get a house, but we tried again. FHA again. I was so afraid. But somebody changed the law, and everything went smoothly."

I didn't tell her that I was the one who changed the law. But I did keep that warm glow with me for a long time.

Again, my purpose was to pass good legislation.

***AH HA!* Changing the law matters to real people.**

The Steve and Brian Bartlett National Champion Longleaf Pine

The "Steve and Brian" national champion pine

Often, your best ideas come from friends at home, and often at unexpected times.

About a year into my first term, I held an all-district town hall. Usually, each town hall would be held in a specific part of the district, like Lake Highlands or North Dallas.

This one was an all-district town hall on a Saturday morning with 250 people in attendance. My constituents were glad to see me, and I was glad to see them.

Most came just to say hello and hear the latest, but I identified several groups who were there with a purpose. That was normal.

One group in particular was the active environmentalists, led by the legendary Ned Fritz. I knew Ned quite well from my city council days.

When I called on him, he briefly described the need for a designated wilderness area in East Texas. But he didn't ask for my vote or support; he simply asked if I would join him to see this wilderness for myself.

I didn't know much about wilderness areas or what that process involved, but I liked to hike in the woods. So I casually answered, "Sure. How about tomorrow at 7:00 a.m.? And I'd like to bring my son Brian along."

Done. In the van on the way to East Texas, with maps and charts spread out, I got an education. And once we were on the ground, I got a graduate education on longleaf pines, the diversity of the forest, carnivorous plants, clear-cut logging, controlled burns, the differences between national parks, national forests, and wilderness areas, and the endangered red-cockaded woodpecker.

Then I learned a hard-to-believe fact: with all of Texas' land, we had only one designated wilderness, and it was in the desert on the New Mexico border.

Ned, who had been working on this for ten years, also described the political land mines and how we might navigate them without too much posturing or anger.

This particular wilderness contained the largest longleaf pine in the nation, the national champion.

It took four years, a lot of twists and turns, and many legislative compromises. Plus, half a dozen more "boots-on-the-ground" hikes in East Texas.

We passed the bill four years later. The following year, Ned's organization named the longleaf pine the "Steve and Brian Bartlett National Champion Longleaf Pine." I still have the photo on my bookshelf of Brian and me leaning against our tree.

My purpose was simple: to preserve 30,000 acres of East Texas wilderness for posterity.

And as a bonus, to walk in the woods with my son Brian.

AH HA! Listen to Ned, and take a walk in the woods.

The Window Screen and the Fire Axe

It was the summer of 1983, and I had passed the previously described amendment to double the funding for public housing repairs.

One day, I looked at my schedule and saw that I was having lunch with the Assistant Secretary of HUD for Public Housing.

Unusual, because I usually didn't have lunch. But it must be important.

"Congressman, I am retiring at the end of the year. Over the past few years, my staff and I have written a bill that would fix the state of public housing dilapidation. Would you like to sponsor it?"

"Huh? What do you mean by 'fix it'? There is not enough money in the whole world to fix it all."

"Actually," he continued, "money is not the problem. The system is designed all wrong. Every major repair requires a separate federal grant, which takes six to ten years. By that time, the building often will have fallen down. Tnd the repairs have to be done by the HUD rule book, which is often wrong and outdated."

"So what is the solution?"

"This bill is designed to fund major repairs like Trammell Crow (one of the largest developers in the U.S., and based in Dallas). Do you know Mr. Crow? Create a reserve fund as part of the operating budget for major repairs. After twenty years, use that reserve fund to make the repairs."

He handed me the four-hundred-page bill, and we shook hands.

It made sense. I confirmed it with one phone call to Trammell Crow's office. Then I went to "Mr. Housing" on the Democratic side, Barney Frank, and asked him to co-sponsor the bill. It made sense to him, too. He said yes, if I would do all the work and warn him when the big-city housing authorities went on the warpath. They lived on federal grants.

It took four painful years. But Barney and I stuck with it.

In the spring of 1987, Henry Gonzales of San Antonio called a markup on a separate housing bill. He hated my reform bill because he loved federal grants.

I came to the markup fifteen minutes early. Mr. Gonzales sent Jerry, his staff guy, over to tell me he would not accept my amendment.

I reached behind my chair and picked up two window screens. "Jerry, these screens came from the San Antonio Housing Authority, given to me by Director Nono Flores. Screen One can be cut with a pocketknife, which I will do in front of the entire committee. See my pocketknife.

"Screen Two cannot be damaged by anything, including a fire axe. See the dent? That dent you see is from a fire axe.

"Screen One is the HUD-required screen. Screen Two has been given to San Antonio (home of Henry Gonzales) by Trammell Crow, which, in the future, would be permitted by my bill in all public housing.

"I will ask the Committee which screen they will vote for."

Henry accepted my bill.

My purpose was to permanently improve the lives of hundreds of thousands of public housing residents.

AH HA! Sometimes you have to show them.

Christmas Eve: War in Panama

Christmas of 1989. President Bush sent the U.S. Army to Panama to arrest the president of Panama, Manuel Noriega, a major drug dealer.

The U.S. military had been reorganized in October 1986, resulting in sweeping reforms that literally created the modern military. I had been a member of the Conference Committee.

On December 23, I had promised Gail I would finally take her Christmas shopping. I arrived home late, around 5:00 p.m. She met me at the door.

"You've got to return this call. It's a constituent, and he needs your help."

"I'll call him from the office tomorrow."

"Not good enough. You call him right now."

Okay. Okay.

I got the man on the phone. "Remember me? I came to your picnic. My wife is from Panama. Her extended family is trapped in a big house in Panama City. The mobs are going house to house, looting and stealing. Help! They're five blocks away."

"What's the address?" I asked. Then I called a secret number at the Pentagon and asked for my friend Dave Gribben, Dick Cheney's Chief of Staff.

I explained the problem. He said, "Hang on."

A moment later: "Colonel, this is Congressman Bartlett." I gave him the address and the name of the family.

Fifteen minutes later, an Army captain knocked on the family's door.

"Sir, Congressman Bartlett in Dallas, Texas, said you have a problem. How can I help?"

The Army secured the house, ran off the mob, and recruited six of the adult family members to come to the police station to serve all night and the next day as emergency bilingual operators.

Purpose, simple: to save a family from the mob.

***AH HA!* Sometimes it just looks easy.**

Refuseniks and the Cold War

It was 1985, the depth of the Cold War. Gail and I led a delegation of Congressmen and their spouses to the Soviet Union to meet with about fifty Refuseniks, most of them waiting to be shipped to labor camps in Siberia for five-year prison sentences, others the wives and children of Refuseniks already in Siberia.

Their crime? Asking permission to leave the Soviet Union. At the time, it was estimated that twenty to thirty thousand people were either in Siberian camps for this "crime" or waiting to be sent.

We attended a Jewish wedding in an apartment in Moscow, presided over by a rabbi flown in from New Jersey. We were there to provide "cover," so the wedding guests were less likely to be arrested by the KGB standing at the door. We were told this was only the second religious wedding in Moscow in decades. Gail clutched her U.S. passport with both hands.

We met a Hebrew teacher who was scheduled for the labor camps in two weeks, cheerfully continuing his lessons.

We visited a nearly empty Orthodox church, where our KGB guide quietly confessed that she sometimes visited alone at midnight to light a candle so no one would know.

We met about four hundred Jews standing in the street outside the empty synagogue on the Sabbath. No one would go inside because they would be put on a "list."

We were followed everywhere by KGB agents, sometimes two or three at a time. We were told to be careful not to lose our followers, because we would be blamed and possibly detained. At one stop, I had to wake up our KGB "tail," who had fallen asleep on a park bench, so we would not lose him.

We met the grandparents of a family in the United States who gave us a photo of the grandchildren they had never met, marked "Born Free." The grandparents were leaving for Siberia the next week. Gail cried.

Aside from the Refuseniks, the Soviet Union was an incredibly depressing place. One example: there were two or three food stores on every block, each with pictures of whatever food was supposed to be in that store. But there was no food. And everyone was always being watched and listened to.

When we returned to the United States, I wrote letters on behalf of every Refusenik I met, and in fact, most of them were eventually allowed to leave. The Soviets do respond to pressure from the U.S.

My purpose was to bring encouragement and secure release for as many as I could.

AH HA! **Would that all could be born free.**

Stick to Your Guns: 5,000 Letters and Phone Calls

In my second term, I prepared an amendment to create a "Supported Employment" section for the reauthorization of Vocational Rehabilitation Agencies. Essentially, this meant providing a job coach or other support to allow someone with a severe disability to work in a job alongside non-disabled employees.

Supported Employment was a proven concept but had not been adopted by Vocational Rehabilitation agencies.

It didn't seem controversial to me. Who could be against disabled workers earning independent, competitive wages?

Answer: the owners of the sheltered workshops, that's who, because they were paying sub-minimum wages.

To my amazement, every member of the Education and Labor Committee, including me, received an average of 5,000 letters, phone calls, and postcards objecting to "The Bartlett Amendment."

Stunned, I went to the committee markup, offered my amendment, and heard a dozen committee members plead with me to withdraw it so they wouldn't have to vote on it.

I listened and said, "Members of the Committee, I am not going to withdraw. And if this amendment is defeated on a voice vote, I will insist on a roll call.

"Anyone who wants to go on the record opposing competitive wages for disabled workers can vote no."

The amendment was adopted 75–0.

My purpose was to create employment for disabled persons.

***AH HA!* When you're right, stick to your guns. And get a roll call.**

Sometimes the Policy Becomes Personal

During my legislative work on disability issues, I learned that early childhood intervention for any child born with a disability is crucial to success. And you can't make it up later. The problem was that most medical professionals and parents didn't know that.

I wanted to see this for myself, so I booked a site visit to Brighton Academy in San Antonio, which specializes in infants with Down syndrome. The results were amazing and quite apparent. Children with Down syndrome receiving early intervention from age one to five were demonstrably more adjusted, happy, and loving in life than those without it.

So, always the one to put a good policy into law, I wrote an Early Childhood bill that mandated hospitals to advise parents of newborns with a disability that early intervention is recommended and to offer specific information on how to access it within three days of childbirth. I attached it to a larger bill going through.

A year later, my best friend, Wick Allison, called from the hospital to tell me his daughter, Chrissy, had been diagnosed with Down syndrome. The pediatrician had advised him to "look for an institution." *AARRRGH!*

Calmly, I said, "Wick, call me in twenty-four hours when you have collected yourself." The next day, after I told him to fire his pediatrician, I explained early intervention and the difference it makes, and how children with Down syndrome can grow into loving, successful, happy adults. I gave him Brighton's contact information.

Six weeks later, Wick's wife, Chris, had gone to Brighton and started early intervention. Chrissy had a wonderful, loving childhood (even took the family car for a joyride at age fourteen) and is today an independent, happy, well-adjusted adult.

Thirty years later, my own grandson Jackson was born totally deaf. We got him cochlear implants on his first birthday, with early intervention therapy for how to hear starting immediately, rather than "waiting until he needs them," as many told us to do. Today, he is an independent, bright, well-adjusted fifteen-year-old.

My purpose was to help Wick raise Chrissy and to provide Jackson with an early start.

AH HA! Politics comes home.

The Cheeseburger Summit: There Are No Secrets in Washington

In 1984, Bilingual Education was up for reauthorization in Federal law. Already pretty controversial. I decided to take it on, with John McCain as my cosponsor. Texas and Arizona. The Bilingual lobby wanted reauthorization with no changes. Opponents wanted to end bilingual education altogether.

John and I had a different plan: renew it and improve it. Include a heavy dose of teaching English.

Sounds simple, but the devil is in the details.

I negotiated directly with the outside lobbies, LULAC and NABE, the largest and toughest Hispanic organizations in Washington.

We went back and forth for months. Finally, we had three issues left. I called the lead lobbyist from LULAC, Arnold Torres, and asked him to come to my office to iron out our differences. He was a tough guy with strong opinions.

He came at noon and I was hungry. I suggested the Rayburn cafeteria for a cheeseburger. Careful to go Dutch treat.

We sat in the middle of the Rayburn cafeteria for over an hour and worked out the language. Now Rayburn cafeteria is big. Usually, three-hundred staff and lobbyists are eating lunch.

Arnold and I shook hands, and I returned to my office.

I was met by my own staff with fear in their eyes. "What have you done? We have received a dozen calls from all over the Hill that you sold out to LULAC for the price of a cheeseburger?"

I called Arnold. He laughed. "Actually, the same thing happened to me. A dozen calls from my people accusing me of selling out for a cheeseburger."

We both stuck with the deal, had a good laugh. Passed the bill with a large bipartisan majority.

Again, the purpose was to help non-English speaking students learn English and get a good education.

***AH HA!* Since there are no secrets in Washington, do everything in the open.**

Tell Bartlett He Ain't Getting No Damn Signature Pen!

But the cheeseburger wasn't the end of the bilingual saga.

By way of background, you should know I collected "signature pens" and letters from the president for the bills I wrote and passed. I have fourteen of them on my office wall. Somewhat of a vanity thing, but passing good legislation was what drove me.

Many of the improvements we made in the bilingual bill were on the conservative side, especially emphasizing the teaching of English. But I knew that would not be good enough for some, so I kept Secretary of Education Bill Bennett informed throughout. He wasn't thrilled about it, but he agreed to the bill.

In the 1984 Reagan campaign, I served as a surrogate campaign speaker in Texas. In September, I did an evening event in San Antonio and had a press conference scheduled in Brownsville at noon the next day, 275 desolate miles south on Highway 281.

There is almost nothing in those 275 miles. The only stop is Three Rivers, a town of about 1,800, roughly halfway.

I stopped at 10:00 a.m. at a saloon in Three Rivers, looking for a cup of coffee. I walked in. The guy behind the bar looked up.

"You the congressman?"

"What? Well, yes."

"The phone's for you."

It was my brilliant and innovative legislative assistant, Becky Campoverde. "You're in trouble. The president is going to veto our bilingual bill. Alan Kranowitz called." Alan was a friend at the White House.

"How'd you find me, Becky?"

"Not hard. Driving from San Antonio to Brownsville, the only place to stop for coffee is Three Rivers, and the saloon is the only place with coffee."

Like I said, she's brilliant.

I called the White House operator. "Get me Alan Kranowitz on the phone."

Alan said, "Nothing you can do. The decision has been made."

"Put your boss, Jim Cicconi, on the phone." Speakerphone, I noted.

"Nothing I can do, Steve. Reagan has always been against bilingual education."

"Jim, can Jim Baker, the White House Chief of Staff, hear me on the speakerphone?"

Gulp. "Well, yes."

"Ask Mr. Baker what I should say at the press conference I'm attending for Reagan in Brownsville in two hours. Brownsville is 80 percent Hispanic. Give me the words, and I'll read them just as you say them."

Silence… a five-count, and no one spoke.

"Okay, we'll sign the bill. But there ain't gonna be no damn signature pen for this one."

And a new purpose: to stare down the chief of staff of the president of the United States.

AH HA! **Timing is everything.**
And always stop for coffee.

Modernizing the Military

One day in the mid-80s, a lobbyist from Dallas-based Texas Instruments came to see me. It was almost a courtesy call rather than a call to action.

Seems U.S. infantry soldiers were equipped with an anti-tank weapon called the Dragon Fly. The problem was that the Dragon Fly was not powerful enough to stop a tank. Worse, a soldier who fired a Dragon Fly would quickly be killed by the tank's .50-caliber machine gun, because the soldier had to guide it to target.

TI was developing a shoulder-fired missile heavy enough to kill a tank, with a fire-and-forget guidance system called AWSM. The procurement had stalled, and TI didn't know why.

"You can't help, Congressman, you're on the wrong committees. But I thought you ought to know."

My dad had been an infantry soldier in World War II and had lost his leg in the Huertgen Forest in 1944, so I had some sympathy for infantry versus tank. I needed corroboration.

I booked myself on a solo NATO tour to the front lines, accompanied by an Army colonel. I told the colonel what I wanted to learn. He arranged a breakfast with the troops in a tent on the border with East Germany. We could see East German soldiers patrolling on their side.

At breakfast, the soldiers ate with loaded carbines in their laps and helmets on their heads. Sitting with a frontline sergeant, I asked about the Dragon Fly.

"I can't tell you what the official policy is, but the Dragon Flies are stored in a warehouse in the next town. If the war starts, my captain has assigned me the task of collecting our requisition of Dragon Flies. Then the captain has ordered me to dump them over the first bridge I come to."

Stunned, I asked why. "Because no soldier would fire them, and if someone tried, he would be dead."

On my return to Washington, I went to see Charlie Wilson, later of *Charlie Wilson's War*. He was not only on the right committee, he was also on the right subcommittee, Military Appropriations.

Six months later, Charlie's staff called to see if I could join him for lunch that day. When I arrived, the chairman of the subcommittee, Jack Murtha, was sitting there with Charlie.

"Steve," said Charlie, "the Dragon Flies are made in Jack's district. We can't just stop cold turkey because jobs are involved. But here is what Jack is willing to do. This year, half the money scheduled for the Dragon Fly will be reassigned to the AWSM. Next year, 70 percent, and the year after, all of it. All you have to do is say yes and keep your damn mouth shut."

Gulp. That's what I did, and the prototype of the AWSM was deployed in Desert Storm, saving the lives of U.S. infantry soldiers and sending the tanks back to Baghdad.

I kept my mouth shut. Until now.

My purpose was clear: to provide weapons to soldiers that could save their lives.

_AH HA!_ Get your facts from a soldier. And talk to the chairman of the committee.

MLK Vote: Steve Don't Do This

And then there are the mistakes.

Confession: I am a workaholic. I've always been a workaholic. Workweeks of eighty to ninety hours were my norm.

So anytime the subject of another paid holiday came up, I was always against it. We already had too many holidays: Columbus Day, Veterans Day, New Year's Day. Posh. Get to work and don't ask me again.

When the Martin Luther King holiday was scheduled for a vote, I didn't spend a minute thinking about it. I admired Reverend King, but we sure didn't need another holiday.

As I left for the floor, I was handed a phone message from Roosevelt Johnson, a friend and well-known African American leader in Dallas. "Tell Steve he should vote for the MLK holiday. This is important for his future."

I entered the House Chamber through the east front doors. Standing there was Mickey Leland, an African American congressman from Houston. He had never asked me for a vote before.

"Steve, how are you going to vote?"

"I can't vote for another holiday, Mickey, not even for Dr. King."

"Steve, don't do this."

Little did I know that six years later, when I announced my run for mayor of Dallas, race relations would be the number one issue facing the city. Everywhere I went, people asked, "Why did you vote against the Martin Luther King holiday?"

No explanation sufficed. I publicly changed my mind, apologized, and sincerely repented. African American voters accepted my apology, and it was sincere, and we moved on. But it was a rough start.

Some things are more important than an extra day of work.

My purpose in avoiding a new holiday was not a noble one.

AH HA! **When a friend gives you deeply felt advice, listen.**

Check the Record to See What Mr. Whitten Said

In 1986, the Democrats added forty seats to their margin, with organized labor as the largest factor. Unions had an agenda of seven major legislative goals, mostly destructive for non-union working Americans, or at least that was my opinion.

And with a seat on the Labor Committee, I was a known leader on labor issues. On the last night of the 1987 session, a big surprise appeared: outlaw double-breasting.

Double-breasting is a long-standing federal policy allowing a contractor who owns multiple subsidiaries, some union and some non-union, to bid on a contract using the most suitable company. It sounds more complicated than it is. Sometimes a union contract is better, and sometimes a non-union contract is.

The bill on the floor would have banned this practice with no hearings, no bill introduced, no debate, and not even a press release. It was the classic Washington "dead of night" attack.

At 6:00 p.m., I received a call from a committee staff member who had been sworn to secrecy. The Appropriations Conference Committee had inserted a surprise rider in the final bill to abolish double-breasting. The bill was scheduled to pass by midnight and go straight to the president.

I walked briskly to the floor to find the principals, about eight of us. Behind the rail, we argued policy, politics, principles, state interests (Mr.

Whitten was from Mississippi), economic damages, House rules, the possibility of a floor amendment, and even a potential presidential veto. I didn't think a veto was likely, but I told them it was a certainty. As I recall, no one dared leave our huddle.

I then asked the Parliamentarian to join us and give his opinion on whether a point of order could be sustained. He said he would take it under advisement.

After five long hours, the Democratic leadership backed down for a combination of practical, policy, political, and procedural reasons.

Jamie Whitten, Chairman of the Appropriations Committee, was handed a one-page amendment, which he offered with unintelligible mumbling. I'm not making that up.

From the Republican microphone, I quickly asked for unanimous consent to dispense with the reading and adopt the amendment. I held my breath.

"So ordered," the Speaker said, and the gavel came down.

I left the House floor through the center doors. Waiting to greet me were a dozen really, really angry union lobbyists who had been working on the strategy for four years.

"Mr. Bartlett, we watched you for five hours from the gallery. Did you just kill the Double-Breasting Amendment?"

"No, I didn't. But you might want to check the record to see what Mr. Whitten had to say."

It occurred to me they might actually throw a punch. Instead, the lobbyist for the Teamsters laughed. "That was the slickest thing I've ever seen done in Congress."

"Thank you," I said.

My purpose, in this case, was to defeat bad legislation.

***AH HA!* Don't leave the House Floor.**
And when in doubt, mumble.

Write Up the Compromise, Joe

We were in the last few days of a Conference Committee on Housing. The base bill was 1,000+ pages long, with dozens of contentious issues, all of which had been ironed out over four weeks of intense negotiations.

One really contentious issue remained: under what circumstances could a city invoke eminent domain with a federally funded project? The law, rules, and court cases were vague, confusing, and often contradictory.

Meaning, of course, yes for a highway, but no for a private shopping center. But what lay in between was not clear.

The two principals were Barney Frank, a liberal Democratic firebrand who was a hard no, and Al D'Amato, a liberal Republican firebrand who represented New York developers who wanted to use eminent domain to acquire property.

Two days before the deadline, neither would budge.

I got a call from Chalmers Wylie, the senior Republican on the Banking Committee.

"Steve, we have a problem, and Henry (Committee Chairman Henry Gonzales) wants you to solve it. You have worked with Barney, and you are a Republican who can talk to Al. Chairman Gonzales wants you to negotiate a compromise."

"Huh? Me?"

"Yes, you. You are the only one who can talk to both."

So I called Committee Staff Director Joe Ventrone, the expert on housing policy in Washington.

"Joe, can this issue be compromised?"

"Sure, I've already drafted the compromise that will give them both what they need," said Joe. He described it to me in general terms, and it sounded reasonable.

"Ok, set up a meeting for the two of us, and Al and Barney. Make it in Al's office to soften him up."

The meeting was in Senator D'Amato's Senate office at 9:00 p.m. Joe and I walked over together.

I didn't describe the compromise; I just said, "Senator, tell me what you are trying to accomplish. Barney, you do the same."

And the fight was on, with curse words in English, Italian, and, I think, Yiddish. Screaming.

I listened, appeared to take notes, and asked a few clarifying questions.

After thirty minutes, they were exhausted.

I then said, "Gentlemen, I think we have an agreement. Joe, can you write this up?"

"Yes, Mr. Bartlett."

We left, and when we got to the Rotunda, Joe stopped and turned to me. "Congressman, what did we just agree to?"

"Why, Joe, they accepted your compromise. First thing in the morning, as if you had been working all night, send it to them and they'll sign it."

And that's what happened. They both "won" and were happy.

And I accomplished my purpose: to pass the bill.

AH HA! **They want to compromise; they just need an excuse to do it.**

Reserving the Right to Object: Taking His Words Down

Even though Henry and I worked together on some things, he still viewed me with suspicion and sometimes anger.

Case in point: another housing bill and a markup in the full Banking Committee. I had prepared an amendment to require HUD to honor the twenty-year contracts with assisted housing developers. "Honor the contract" seems like a lay-down case.

But the bill before us unilaterally canceled the key terms of these contracts. Henry's bill.

I knew I needed eight Democrats to pass an amendment to delete the cancellation. I easily rounded up the first six. I then went to Ben Erdreich, a mild-mannered Democrat from Alabama who seldom spoke in committee or voted with Republicans. And he brought another Democrat with him.

As soon as I introduced the amendment and Ben spoke for it, Henry went ballistic. Henry could count, and he knew if Ben was for it, the amendment would pass.

He immediately began castigating Ben. And then he went too far.

"AND NOW, YOU HAVE MADE A DEAL WITH THE DEVIL INCARNATE!"

Pointing at me.

Calling a Member the "devil incarnate" or any other derogatory name is a violation of the "non-disparagement" House rule. And the penalty is draconian: physical removal from the Capitol for twenty-four hours. That's front-page stuff, especially since Henry, well known as a pugilist, would not have left willingly. The Sergeant-at-Arms might even have arrested him.

I quietly turned on my red light, seeking recognition.

The one hundred fifty staff members, press, and lobbyists in the room drew in their breath and did not exhale.

The aforementioned Joe Ventrone got in my left ear, "Don't do it, Mr. Bartlett, don't do it." And Jerry, Henry's staff member, was shouting in Henry's ear, "Apologize, Mr. Chairman. Apologize!"

Rather than making my objection (known as "taking the gentleman's words down"), I quietly reserved my right. And under my reservation, I could speak as long as I wanted.

I spoke quietly, softly, and kindly. I stated that I believed the gentleman from Texas, my colleague and friend, was honorable and meant no harm. And if he would apologize, I would withdraw my reservation.

After a long five minutes of my monologue, Henry issued the key words, "I apologize."

I withdrew my reservation, and the crisis was averted.

In this case, **my purpose was not to embarrass Henry. It was to quietly insist on decorum.**

AH HA! **Load your gun, but don't pull the trigger.**

I Object!

On the other hand, I recall several times when it was time to actually "object" rather than "reserve the right to object."

The first time was in a joint subcommittee hearing with the Labor Standards and Environmental Oversight Committees. An odd combination, so I knew something was up.

It was chaired by the feared, "take no prisoners" George Miller of California.

Several officials at the EPA, late in the Reagan Administration, were accused by a reporter of having dinner with energy industry lobbyists. Not illegal, but unseemly, and they shouldn't have done it.

These three junior-level officials were scheduled to testify on a few policy issues. It was clear to me they were being set up, and they didn't see it coming. Miller planned to get them to give conflicting testimony and have them indicted for perjury.

Well, actually, Miller's staff told my staff, who told me the game plan.

Opening the hearing, he asked them to stand and then mumbled, "Ask unanimous consent that the witnesses be sworn in. Raise your right hand."

Unanimous consent? "I OBJECT."

"I have never seen witnesses required to take the oath. They were clearly neither advised nor prepared to do so."

Now, under the House Rules, Miller could recess the hearing, move to the House Floor to debate for three hours, have one or more roll call votes, and then return to the hearing. By that time, the witnesses would have sought counsel and prepared. Or he could just proceed to ask them questions.

He uncharacteristically backed down, and while the witnesses shortly thereafter resigned, they didn't go to prison.

A more dramatic moment came during the middle of the first Gulf War, at 10:30 p.m., while debating an appropriations bill, with three hundred Members milling around. Joe Kennedy was recognized to speak for five minutes. Joe and I usually disagreed, but we were friends.

He proceeded on a rant, tearing into the military, our troops, and President Bush, alleging war crimes and worse in the conduct of the war. All without a shred of evidence and totally unrelated to the appropriations bill under consideration. Apparently, no one was listening except yours truly.

At the end of his five minutes, he asked for unanimous consent to proceed for another five minutes.

There's that unanimous consent again.

"I OBJECT," I said loudly, standing from my seat. It was like a Paine Webber commercial. All sounds stopped. Three hundred Congressmen stared at me.

Joe demanded to know who objected. "The gentleman from Texas," pointing at me.

Furious, Joe bounded to where I was standing.

In my face, nose to nose with clenched fists, "Why did you object? I thought we were friends."

"We are friends, Joe, but I wanted you to stop talking," I said with a big smile.

And that was my simple purpose.

I thought he was going to hit me, but then he realized it was kinda funny.

"Okay. Okay. Let's go have a beer."

AH HA! **Sometimes just object, and stay friends.**

Che Guevara?

Friends or not, partisanship is always there in Washington. But somehow, the work gets done.

One of the traditions in Washington is that when a new Administration comes in, the appointees from the previous Administration try to keep their heads down and carry on.

Ronald Reagan was elected in 1980. By 1983, most of the political appointees at the Department of Education had been replaced by the Reagan administration. (This does not include civil service employees, only presidential appointees.)

In the summer of 1983, we had a hearing on the reauthorization of the Women's Educational Equity Act. Not something you want to mess with, but the office should have been aligned with the current Administration.

The aforementioned Becky Campoverde learned that the holdover director had a life-sized poster of Che Guevara on the door of her office at the Department of Education. Che represented neither women, nor education, nor equity.

Somehow, this director had stayed on long after Reagan took office.

Everyone was tiptoeing around the question of why she was still there until my turn.

"Madam Director, I have one simple question—well, two: Do you have a full-sized poster of Che Guevara in your office at the Department of Education? And why?"

She resigned the next week. And we did reauthorize the Act. With a new director.

In hindsight, it was kind of a small purpose: to take Che Guevara's poster down from the Department of Education.

***AH HA!* Be careful whose pictures you hang on your wall.**

Back Home, the World Was About to Collapse

During my time in Congress, the Dallas and Texas economies crashed. From 1985 to 1989, Texas suffered through the savings and loan crisis, a massive economic collapse.

I had heard rumors in the fall of 1984. Mike Myers, a wealthy real estate developer and banker, came to a UT/OU party in October with a big smile, announcing he had "just gone to cash." I didn't know exactly what that meant, but it sounded ominous.

Two weeks later, I ran into John Stuart, a longtime friend and the new CEO of Capital Bank, on a sidewalk in Austin. "Steve, glad to run into you. I had planned to call you next week. Need to warn you, everything is about to crash. Be prepared, but you can't stop it."

Huh? Huh? Huh?

So in December 1984, I went to the man with the biggest window on the economy in Texas: the CEO of Republic Bank. Republic was the largest oil lender in Texas. Out of respect for his otherwise exemplary service, I will not share his name. Republic officers Joe and Bill (both friends of mine) and my District Director, Lisa Stoltenberg, were also in the meeting.

We started with a little small talk, then I got to the point.

"I've been hearing rumors that the economy is at risk, especially related to oil. My question is this: oil prices have declined from a peak of $31 to

$28. When Republic Bank makes a business loan, what assumption about oil prices do you make?"

He laughed and did a side glance at Bill and Joe. Not a good sign.

"Well, Steve, I hate to tell you this, but Bill, our economist here, has done a supply and demand study, and he concluded that oil could go down to, what did you say, Bill, $12 a barrel."

"But we know that's not going to happen. So if oil goes below $20 a barrel, Congress will intervene and put a floor at $20."

Thinking of Ronald Reagan's free market convictions and Congress's deep antipathy toward Texas, I was speechless.

In Texas at the time, oil was the basis of the economy, real estate was based on oil, and the banks depended on real estate.

I was dizzy. Afraid. Petrified.

Lisa, sensing I was about to say something very impolitic, announced I was late and hustled me out. When we got outside, I literally threw up at the curb. I mean, I actually vomited.

Oil eventually bottomed at $10. Real estate collapsed. Home prices dropped 40 percent. Every single big bank in Texas, including Republic, failed, as did 225 smaller banks.

Happening simultaneously was a massive real estate crash, fueled by massive Savings and Loan fraud, leading to an oversupply of housing, followed by a collapse. A worse economic depression in Texas than even the Great Depression of the 1930s.

I returned to Washington and tried to help, but it was a total collapse.

I had no purpose that could succeed.

_AH HA!_ The laws of supply and demand are immutable.

The White House Operator is Your Friend

One of the little-known but effective tools in Washington is access to the White House Operator. Pete Madigan, the Legislative Assistant I hired for three months to "teach me the ropes," introduced me to its availability.

By calling the White House Operator, a congressman can get any political appointee on the phone any time, day or night. Hard to believe, and I suspect only those in Leadership (Pete had been Floor Assistant to a member of Leadership) use the access, as most Members don't know about it.

The secrets are: be polite, be confident, be specific about who you want to reach, and let your tone of voice carry your expectation.

And most importantly, don't abuse it, or they will cut you off.

I used the White House Operator several times to place calls. I already described my bilingual education dust-up with James Baker.

Once I was on the Floor of the House on the last night of the Session, about 11:00 p.m. My East Texas Wilderness Act (remember Ned Fritz) was pending. I had worked on this legislation for four years and had agreement from all sides.

Then the White House Liaison told me the bill had not been cleared by the Assistant Secretary of Agriculture, who was out of town.

"White House Operator, please get me Assistant Secretary X on the phone right away." She tracked him down somewhere out West. I introduced myself and explained the situation.

"Oh yes, I remember that. Yes, we are okay with that bill." I handed the phone to the Republican floor director, who listened and just said, "Good to go."

Another time, on the last night of the Session, I was negotiating a key provision of a Housing Bill with my old nemesis, Henry Gonzales. He and his staff had rejected all my well-reasoned arguments.

I found Chalmers Wylie, Ranking Republican of the Committee, having dinner in the Capitol Dining Room. It was about 8:00 p.m.

I explained my strategy. "Chalmers, we need Henry to think the bill is at risk of a veto if he doesn't accept this change. So I'm going to get Howard Baker, White House Chief of Staff, on the phone, and you need to ask him to not be available if Henry Gonzales calls him tonight."

Chalmers said, "How are you going to do that?"

I dialed the White House Operator. "Please get me Howard Baker on the phone for Congressman Wylie and Congressman Bartlett."

Done.

Howard said, "Chalmers, happy to accommodate. I won't be available until tomorrow morning."

Done, and done.

My purpose was to pass good legislation with a simple phone call.

AH HA! **You have to know who to call, and call them.**

What'd You Do, Read the Damn Bill?

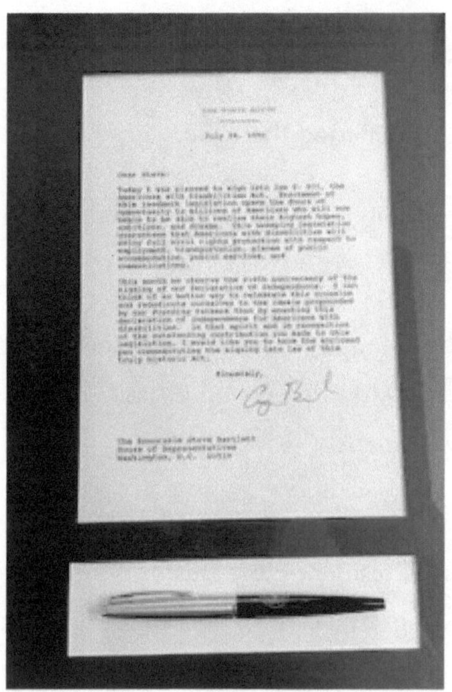

Signature Pen for ADA

And then came 1989. George Bush, the Americans with Disabilities Act, and, in a way, the culmination of all I had done in Congress for eight years.

I had written and passed a half dozen disability-focused bills, all with the same theme: bringing independence to the lives of disabled persons. Each bill was a piece of the puzzle, but none were comprehensive.

I was a known leader on disability issues, a bona fide Reagan Conservative, and I had developed legislative skills.

There had been quiet talk for a few years about a comprehensive civil rights law for disabled Americans, bringing together transportation, employment, housing, and public accommodations. It would not be easy.

And it was complicated. And it could be costly.

But only a handful understood the issue.

Then we got lucky: George H. W. Bush understood disability issues and civil rights.

The night before his Inaugural, over one thousand disability advocates, led by Texan Justin Dart, I'm proud to say, held a massive reception honoring the new president.

And George Bush delivered. Boyden Gray, White House counsel, nudged me: "Listen to this." President-elect Bush announced to the nation that he would send to Congress a civil rights bill for disabled Americans. Tears of joy, wailing and screaming, and a few people passed out.

That was the easy part. As I said, it was complicated: four committees and seven subcommittees, and every trade group in Washington had to be assuaged.

Working with House Democrat Steny Hoyer, I was designated the House Republican leader to bring it home. This was literally new law, with no blueprint to go on.

We met weekly, then daily, going through every page (1,500 pages) line by line, and then back to the committees of jurisdiction. Steny's staff reported that he and I spent over 100 hours in these sessions.

And we brought in disparate interests to sit in the room with us: the U.S. Chamber of Commerce, the major disability groups, transit, housing, and restaurant groups, the Labor Policy Association, the Leadership Conference on Civil Rights, and often the White House. Ralph Neas, the executive director of the U.S. Leadership Conference on Civil Rights, was particularly helpful, as was prominent civil rights attorney Chai Feldblum.

Without understating the intensity, let's just say there were sharp elbows everywhere.

When we were done, the bill passed nearly unanimously in the Senate and 380–35 in the House. The bill signing was on the South Lawn with 5,000 in attendance.

I hate to bring it up, but one funny little thing happened on the way to passage. It was a Friday afternoon, and Patricia Morrissey came into my office smiling. "Here is the final bill, ready to go to print. Fifteen hundred pages and eighteen months of my life. I'm ready for a stiff drink and a good night's sleep."

I handed it back. "Pat, find the section that exempts Congress from complying with the ADA."

"What? They wouldn't do that!"

"Yes, they would. Find it."

Sunday at 3:30 p.m., Pat called. "You were right. It's on page 719. Can I have a drink now?"

First thing Monday morning, I called Steny. "Steny, this is Steve. Page 719."

Long silence. "What did you do, read the damn bill?" Steny explained he was not the problem, his orders had come from "higher up."

We got the Congressional exemption out, and the ADA became law. And that law changed the face of America, profoundly.

My purpose, for eight years, was to allow persons with disabilities to live independent lives, including employees and visitors at the U.S. Congress.

AH HA! **Important things take time. And always read the damn bill.**

Take Time to Clear Your Mind

I will close this section with something personal and profound.

When I turned forty, in my third term in Congress, I was still running on all sixteen cylinders. Intense, focused, and a committed workaholic. Working 7:00 a.m. to 9:00 p.m. Monday through Thursday. Then flying to Dallas and working a full schedule until Saturday night at about 6:00 p.m.

I was going to save America with my personal efforts.

But I noticed I began to be distracted, to daydream, and my mind wandered. I actually went to my doctor for a brain scan. (Came out fine.)

But I couldn't shake the feeling that something was wrong. I asked Gail, and she said, "Well, you do seem a little distracted. In fact, you have been a total jerk lately."

So I enrolled in an eight-day Outward Bound course in the Boundary Waters of northern Minnesota. Intense challenges, both physical and mental. Two days before the end is the Solo. They put you on a rock by yourself with no one else in the vicinity for twelve hours.

Told to think about your life.

That's when I figured it out. What I was daydreaming about was outdoor experiences — hikes, backpacks, horseback trips, rafting. And my frustration was that I had trapped myself into believing I did not have time for such foolishness.

And then I discovered, right there in my own brain, that I did have time, if I planned it. Put an outdoor trip on my annual schedule, just like a legislative hearing, a town hall, a convention, or election day.

And better yet, no one really wanted to see me during the August recess or between Christmas and New Year's.

Of course, Gail and my family might.

I rushed home to Gail. "Darling, I figured it out, but I can't fix it without your permission. If you will let me take an annual outdoor adventure, I will promise to take the family on a one-week annual vacation every year.

"And I will be more of a human being when I come home."

Done and done. My first trip was a week off-trail in the million-acre John Muir Wilderness. And I have not missed a year since. After Congress and City Hall, I sometimes did two or three a year.

And that's how I regained my life balance. And saved my marriage. Both noble purposes.

***AH HA*! You know the answer, sit on a rock and figure it out. And then have the courage and permission from a good spouse, to act on it.**

LEAVING CONGRESS FOR CITY HALL: THE CAMPAIGN

Why Leave A Safe Place for a Firestorm? Carpe Diem

I am often asked, "Why would you leave a safe Congressional seat for City Hall? I mean, that is an impossible job, and in Congress, anything is possible."

The short answer: I had concluded, with considerable evidence, that the Dallas city government was broken. Fistfights at City Hall (between council members and public speakers), racial anger overflowing, and violent crime increasing every month. Downtown was shrinking fast, with virtually no new employers moving into Dallas proper. White flight and jobs were fleeing to the suburbs, and the city had lost two lawsuits in the prior year that cost $500 million each. On average, there were seven fatal police shootings of citizens per year, and an equal number of police officers killed by gunfire.

And worse, the various public interests had virtually given up. People regularly told me it could not be fixed. The most common refrain in conversations about downtown was, "Would the last person to leave downtown please turn out the lights?"

Dallas had given up any belief that things could be turned around.

In fact, one of the campaign slogans that tested really high among white voters was "Believe Again!" The only problem was that Black voters were fine with the "Believe" part, but asked, "What do you mean, 'Again?'"

Again? Sounds like, "Go back to the good old days of Ozzie and Harriet" (actual quotes from internal focus groups). Back to no voice at City Hall, back to no mortgages in African American neighborhoods, back to failing schools. Of course, we already had those things, but the African American community didn't want to go back to even worse days.

So we kept the "Believe" and dropped the "Again." We made it "Believe in Bartlett." Put it on yard signs and t-shirts. A bit tacky, I thought, but it had a nice alliteration, and our volunteers loved it.

I realized that Dallas could recover, but it would take someone to lead, a change agent, and more importantly, someone to show Dallas how to believe in herself again.

Someone else could have done it, but none who could have succeeded were running, or even rumored to be running. After surveying the field, conferring with Gail and a few close friends, I decided to take the leap.

Of course, that was my opinion, and the other candidates were fine, honorable people. But the decision to resign from Congress and run for mayor was mine alone.

To accomplish my purpose of putting Dallas on the right track, I had to resign from Congress and get elected as mayor.

"Burn the boats," as Cortez said as he departed for the interior.

AH HA! **Burn the boats.**

You Know I'm a Black Guy, Right?

First up on the agenda was race. Racial tension, distrust, and anger were everywhere. Somewhere along the way, Dallas had bypassed the whole civil rights and inclusive politics that other cities had gotten right: Atlanta, Houston, Tampa, Los Angeles, and even Chattanooga.

It wasn't for lack of trying, but Dallas was long on appearance: tri-chairmen of everything, quotas for minority contracting, lots of speeches and nice words, but no real substance. Mostly well-meaning window dressing. The Whites resented it, and the African Americans didn't believe anything was changing.

My second imperative was to organize a first-rate campaign, with leadership that knew what they were doing and trusted me.

So my first action was to select and empower a Campaign Chairman: Calvin Stephens, an African American businessman I had known and trusted for twenty years. Likable, really smart, firm, empathetic leadership style. No hidden motives.

Consulting only with Jim Oberwetter and Martha Weisend, the Co-Chairman and a well-known Reagan Republican, I asked Calvin to dinner. Chili's on I-30 in Southeast Dallas.

We sat down and each ordered a big glass of tea. Calvin looked at his watch and said he couldn't stay long; it was his daughter's birthday. He then said, "I'm for you, and I will do anything you want me to: yard signs, phone banks, Southeast Dallas Co-Chairman, anything."

So I charted out the org chart on a Chili's napkin, starting at the bottom of the pyramid. He looked puzzled. When I finished, and his name was nowhere to be seen, I wrote his name at the top. "That's you, Calvin, the Campaign Chairman."

He stared in shock, I mean, in absolute shock. He then knocked over his big glass of tea. He blurted out, "You know I'm a Black guy, right?!!" I mean, he actually said those words.

After we cleaned up the mess, he said, "Steve, you've been out of Dallas too long. The Black guy is the Co-Chairman, or maybe the Tri-Chairman, to include Hispanics. The real Chairman is the White guy. That's the way Dallas works. No African American has ever been the real chairman of anything."

"Calvin, we are out to change that. You are the Chairman. The real Chairman. And to make sure everyone gets the message, you will also be the official Treasurer, so your name will be on every piece of campaign material, from yard signs to mailings. And you will sign the checks."

"I hope you know what you're doing," Calvin replied.

Calvin was a superb Chairman. Indeed, a major reason I won. And that was my purpose.

AH HA! **If you are going to change, start at the top!**

Bringing S. M. Wright to North Dallas

This *AH HA!* story fits in the context of Calvin Stephens, racial tension, and the earlier section on my mistaken vote against the Martin Luther King Jr. Holiday. So here goes.

Dallas was largely still segregated. North Dallas meant White, South Dallas meant Black, West Dallas meant Hispanic, and East Dallas meant older population.

When I announced, the most prominent African American leader in Dallas was Reverend S. M. Wright, Pastor of the People's Baptist Church in South Dallas and titular head of the Interdenominational Ministerial Alliance, which included all the Black ministers in Dallas. Since the 1950s, S. M. had a comfortable relationship (some thought too comfortable) with the Dallas Citizens Council, the powerful business establishment. S. M. delivered the church vote for establishment candidates and bond issues, and the Citizens Council delivered money for the churches and good projects in South Dallas. Both sides "kept the peace."

So before I announced, S. M. was asked what he thought. He was firm. "We'll go along with a lot, but we are not going to have a mayor who voted against the Martin Luther King Jr. holiday. Not gonna have it."

Couldn't have been clearer. Calvin asked S. M. if he would meet with me. Reluctantly, he agreed.

I waited in his outer office for an hour. I sincerely apologized, as I had done publicly. Not enough. So I asked to meet with the Alliance, where I also apologized and quoted the Bible. No excuses. I was wrong. They were polite but held the line: no way.

But that was early in the campaign. My issues of racial diversity, justice, stopping violent crime, fairness, and good jobs in all parts of Dallas started to sink in. And they started to listen. I kept to the same message in North Dallas as in South Dallas, and that resonated.

I included stops at Black churches in my weekly routine and met with pastors of other Black churches. I paid my respects and kept it humble. The word got back to S. M.

At long last, he endorsed me from the pulpit.

But that's not the end of the story. In the last week of the campaign, we still had to close the racial gap, particularly in North Dallas, where White voters were fearful that I would not be accepted by African Americans and that we would have more racial tension.

Calvin went to S. M., and he agreed to tape a thirty-second TV spot. He had a very distinctive voice. And, to the point, putting the voice with S. M.'s full-screen photo in a last-week TV spot aimed at White voters in North Dallas.

Wow. The iconic S. M. Wright had been endorsing candidates from the pulpit in South Dallas since the 1950s, but he had never been invited to speak to White audiences in North Dallas.

My Kitchen Cabinet, about ten very bright political minds, met at midnight at the TV studio. Dissent. Raised voices. Conflicting opinions. High risk.

After an hour, Calvin, the Chairman, spoke. Calvin had never been authoritarian, but this night, he quietly said,

"You've each had your say, and we've listened to each other. But tonight, on this issue, it's my call. We are letting S. M. Wright come to North Dallas. We are running the spot."

I'm convinced the S. M. Wright TV spot won the election. And Calvin Stephens won S. M. Wright.

To accomplish my purpose, I had to win on both sides of town.

***AH HA!* Stay humble, apologize when you are wrong, and say the same thing on both sides of town.**

THE MAYOR YEARS

Throwing Chairs: Where Do I Start?

So it was a long, arduous campaign, from March to November. I answered every question, but at every appearance, I focused on three imperatives: reduce violent crime, create more jobs in Dallas, and bring peace to City Hall.

While I acknowledged there were other problems to be solved, I stated that if we didn't solve those three, nothing else would matter.

I shared earlier a description of the lack of decorum, racial anger, the tension and name-calling on the city council, the fistfights in the council chambers, and the consistent tone of anger and disruptive behavior.

Indeed, my opening gambit was to write a proposed new set of rules for the council and say I would introduce them at my first council meeting, insisting on a roll-call vote. I called it "The Peace Plan." I challenged each of my opponents to sign it. Of course, they didn't. So any time one of them launched a negative attack on me, I would shake my head sorrowfully and say, "Well, I see why you didn't sign the peace plan."

After the election, there was one more meeting of the city council before I was to take office. I attended as a spectator, front and center.

At one point, one of the council members got so angry at the others that he stood up and threw his metal stool (he sat on an elevated metal stool) at the other council members.

His name was Al Lipscomb. He was the radical version of S. M. Wright, a long-time, angry civil rights leader in Dallas. He had called me a racist publicly when I announced.

On my first council day as mayor, I asked that Al be named mayor pro tempore. He was stunned but came over and sat next to me in the mayor pro tempore chair.

It was a long day, but after about two hours, he leaned over and whispered, "Mayor, you know who I am and what I do, right?"

"Yes, Al, I do."

"Well, why did you make me mayor pro tempore?"

"So you won't have as far to throw the chair." I smiled broadly.

There was a good ten-second pause, and then he also smiled broadly, and we shook hands.

Al was the picture of decorum for the rest of his term. And that was my purpose

AH HA! **Better to make a friend than get hit by a chair.**

Set the Mission in Clear, Unmistakable Terms

his agenda

Mayor-elect to focus on safety, prosperity

By David Jackson

ELECTIONS '91

- How state issues fared
- Whitmire leaves legacy of change
- Term limits drive to continue
- Hispanic support helped Bartlett
- Mayoral results by precinct
- New Dallas City Council members
- Layoffs possible for crossing guards
- Totals on Dallas races, issues
- Anti-incumbent sentiment across U.S.
- Gramm catches flak over Pennsylvania

First day as mayor

Good start on peace at City Hall. Now turning to violent crime.

First, a word about Dallas' council–manager form of government. The mayor in Dallas has no management authority. None. All employees, including the handful in the mayor's office, work for the city manager.

But I did have several "powers," the chief among them being to set the mission so that everyone wants to achieve the goal. Then measure the success and praise profusely.

I had a few weeks to write my Inaugural Address. This was a big deal, with several thousand people and lots of media in attendance.

I deliberately set the mission. "We will reduce the number of violent crimes in all four categories: murder, rape, robbery, and aggravated assault within one year."

Now, to give you an idea of how bold this mission was, Dallas had experienced an increase in violent crime in all four categories every month for twenty years. Hadn't missed a month or a category.

I sent the draft to the City Manager for comment. She sent it back as, "We will attempt to decrease the rate of increase in crime during the next four years."

I sent it back with the original language. She replied with more watered-down suggestions.

Two days before the Inaugural, I told her, "Jan, this is what I am going to say in these words." She replied that it couldn't be done. I replied, "Well then, I guess we will both be thrown out in four years."

A few years later, Assistant City Manager A. C. Gonzales told me the Command Chiefs met two days after the Inaugural, and they were quite despondent because they believed this could not be done. A. C. simply said, "Well, the mayor has promised it, so why don't we at least give it a try? Nothing to lose."

Over the course of two weeks, they came up with a plan: hot spot patrols, bicycle and horseback patrols, expedited judicial hearings, cops with binoculars, and much more.

But the piece that made it work was something the Chief said: "Mayor, you know what police like more than anything?"

Answer: "Overtime."

So the Chief identified the 600 officers with the highest rate of felony arrests and the lowest number of citizen complaints. Paid them overtime. The Chief told them to arrest felons and be courteous when they did it. "If you have a single citizen complaint, I'm taking you off overtime and sending you back to patrol."

Six hundred forty-seven felony arrests in six weeks without a single citizen complaint.

There was a lot more to it than that, but that was the start. And we reduced the number of violent crimes in all categories in five months, and every month thereafter. And the City started to believe in itself again.

First step in purpose: make a big reduction in violent crime.

_AH HA!_ Set the mission in clear, unmistakable terms!

Imminent Danger of Death or Serious Bodily Injury

These words have power. I learned them as Chair of the Committee on Model Rules for Law Enforcement. See chapter entitled "The Byrd Rule."

Dallas not only had a violent crime problem, but we also had an excessive force problem. And they were related. Because if the public perceives that the police will shoot first, then too often a civilian will shoot first. Violence begets violence.

Over the prior several years, Dallas had averaged seven police killings of civilians per year and seven civilian killings of police officers. In one case, an eighty-year-old woman in South Dallas called 911 about 11:00 p.m. to report a prowler. She sat on her front porch with a .22 single-shot rifle in her lap to wait.

When police arrived, they stood in the street and shouted for her to "put down the gun." Confused and with bad eyesight, she did nothing.

They shot her dead. Neither officer was disciplined.

I did not know what to expect of the new police chief, Bill Rathburn, but I quickly learned he had the right stuff. I asked him an open-ended question: "Chief, how can we stop the police-civilian shootings?"

He was prepared. "Mayor, we have to retrain the entire police department, top to bottom, on the use of deadly force. It's called imminent danger of death or serious bodily injury, or keep your weapon in its holster. And I will enforce that relentlessly."

Wow. Music to this mayor's ears. "Chief, the current policy of DPD is that in the event of a police shooting, they wait for the Grand Jury. If there's no indictment (and there is never an indictment), the police officer is kept on the force."

Chief Rathburn made direct eye contact. "That's not my policy. I will investigate every case within days, and if excessive force was used, I will fire the officer. Immediately."

"What can I do to help?"

"One thing. If I fire them, don't reinstate them. Every disciplinary action taken in the past three years has been overturned by the city's civil service commission, and the officer has been returned to the street with pay."

I kept my part of the bargain. I appointed Jaime Ramon, a highly regarded employment lawyer, as chairman of the civil service commission. "Jaime, if the Chief has fired a police officer for excessive force and you hear information that bothers you in the hearing, then tell the Chief what you learned. Otherwise, keep the officer fired. And I don't want to read about it in the newspaper."

Chief Rathburn went personally to every shift change in the eight substations. (That's twenty-four appearances in a little over a week) "Officers, you have a new Chief. The new standard is that if you fire your weapon in the absence of imminent risk of death or serious bodily injury, I will fire you within forty-eight hours. And the new mayor has told me he will keep you fired."

Chief Rathburn stated his purpose clearly.

From that moment, there was not another shooting of a civilian by a police officer or of a police officer by a civilian during my term. And for several years thereafter.

Not one.

Purpose: stop shooting innocent people.

AH HA! Imminent risk of death or serious bodily injury

Saving Mobil

A couple of weeks after the election, and before I took office, I got a call from Rick Douglas, president of the Chamber of Commerce. Side note: Rick is a lifelong friend and one of the true stalwarts in civic circles in Dallas.

"Bad news," said Rick. "We have been summoned to meet with the CEO of Mobil at his office in Fairfax, Virginia. ASAP."

Mobil was the largest and most prominent employer in downtown Dallas, and downtown had been losing corporations rapidly for a decade. In fact, Mobil symbolized downtown. The Flying Red Horse had a beacon atop a skyscraper, visible for fifty miles.

Rick, John Adams (the chamber chairman), and I traveled together. Alan Murray, the CEO, was courteous but firm. "We are closing our offices downtown and sending our thousand employees elsewhere in one year, so you can prepare. When would you like to announce it?"

I took out an index card and a pen.

"What would we have to do to change this decision?"

"First, our employees (he actually said 'secretaries') would have to tell us they feel safe during their lunch hour.

"Second, the cross-town traffic to and from our building is a nightmare.

"Third, street crime in downtown has to go to zero. We have to feel safe and be safe."

I wrote it down and put the card in my pocket.

"If we accomplish those things by July, will you stay?"

Long staring contest. He finally said, "Of course."

On the way to the airport, Rick whispered to me, "How the hell are you going to pull that off, Mayor?"

"With extreme urgency," was my reply.

The "secretaries feeling safe" was the easiest. The problem was that homeless men were drinking on city sidewalks and acting aggressively. In my second week, I asked the council to outlaw drinking in public in downtown. I then privately coached the city attorney to seek a quick verdict on the lawsuit to overturn our ordinance and to expedite an appeal at the Fifth Circuit, which promptly upheld our ordinance.

Chief Rathburn personally made the first arrest in front of TV cameras. Drinking on downtown sidewalks stopped. Nobody wants to go to jail.

Two months later, I met with the employees at Mobil, and they told me they suddenly felt safe.

Traffic was also easy. The City Transportation Department re-engineered cross-town traffic patterns. Duh.

Then I privately said to Bill Rathburn, our amazing Chief of Police, "Chief, you have six months to get to zero crime in downtown Dallas. Do what you have to do."

He assigned seventy-five officers to downtown, reporting to his best Deputy Chief. We had horseback patrols, bicycle patrols, foot patrols, and high-powered binoculars atop the skyscrapers with radios to the ground.

Eating lunch at a café in the Farmers Market area of downtown a few months later, I observed two officers on bicycles chasing and easily catching a purse snatcher. I went outside and asked what happened. The officer pointed to the top of a downtown skyscraper, where another officer stood waving.

Within three months, street crime in downtown was literally at zero.

On July 1, I called Alan Murray. "We did what we said we would do."

Amazingly, he was prepared. "Actually, Mayor, I was expecting your call. I've talked to my people on the ground, and they confirmed it. We'll stay."

Purpose accomplished: Keep Mobil.

Mobil did move out about fifteen years later, but for economic reasons. And by that time, Dallas was on a roll, and it didn't matter that much.

_AH HA!_ Identify the problem and solve it.

Zero is a Very Small Number

The next step was how to bring employers back to downtown. The stalwart Rick Douglas had reorganized the Dallas Chamber to create a City of Dallas economic development division and assigned his top professionals to it.

In mid-December, he and I convened a meeting of the City and Chamber economic development staff. About fourteen of them, as I recall.

I had a pretty good idea why employers were moving out. But who was moving in, and why? I thought we could use that data to build on success.

"How many employers have moved in?" Blank stares. So it was a short meeting. I asked them to reconvene in a week with an answer.

A week later: "Mayor, as you know, downtown has lost 100,000 employees in the last ten years. But we cannot find a single employer that has moved into downtown in ten years."

Gulp. Sinking feeling in the pit of my stomach. Not one?

I sat down and quietly said, "Zero. Is. A. Very. Small. Number."

"There are fourteen of you. Your job in the next two weeks is to sell. Return to your offices and cold call every business list you can find. Los Angeles, New York, Chicago, Cedar Rapids, anywhere with a phone book. Come back in two weeks."

Two weeks later, we reconvened. "Mayor, we have one. It's small, but they want to move to downtown."

It was a chiropractor's office with five chiropractors and five staff. Ten employees.

They moved in a month later. We declared their opening day "Dallas Chiropractor Day." Put banners on streetlight poles on Main Street. Press conference with TV cameras, many speeches.

And I got a back massage on camera for the 6:00 p.m. news.

As I left, the owner pulled me aside to ask, "Mayor, do you do this for all your new businesses?" I didn't have the heart to tell him he was it. I just smiled and said yes.

The next week, we announced a 400-employee regional advertising agency moving to downtown Dallas. And later that year, a 300-person call center. And we were on the road to turning it around.

Purpose: bring new employers to downtown Dallas.

AH HA! **The first one is the hardest.**

West End Breakfast

Now to connect the dots: more crime means less economic development. Fewer crimes bring back business.

In December, I was called by some very despondent and angry Dallasites: the merchants of the West End.

The West End was an area of bars, restaurants, and retail in converted warehouses in the southwest corner of downtown Dallas. They were just getting started in 1980 when I was on the council. I helped them get a special zoning designation. Ten years later, I assumed all was going well.

Wrong.

I could see by the look on their faces when I walked in for breakfast that things were very, very, very wrong.

"Mayor, we are all going out of business. Some shops have already closed and left. A year from now, none of us will be here. None. Of. Us."

Stunned, I asked, "What's wrong?"

The short answer was crime. Lots of it, and constant. Muggings, assaults, a few rapes every month, and even an occasional murder.

But the long answer was this: "Your police department says they can't do anything about it. They say it's random criminals, and all they can do is respond to 911."

I felt my blood boiling. "Do you have the crime stats?"

"Oh yes," they said, and showed me the record for the last year. A steady increase in crime every week. Every single week.

And retail sales were down 40 percent in one year.

I said, "Will you meet me back here for breakfast next Tuesday?"

Back at City Hall, I insisted on a meeting with Chief Rathburn that day. I showed him the stats and a map of the West End. My jaw was set, and I didn't smile.

He quickly agreed on a plan. He would assign a Three-Star Deputy Chief to the West End. He would have twenty-five uniformed cops stationed there—some on foot, some on horseback, most on bicycles. The Deputy Chief would personally meet for breakfast with the merchants every Tuesday.

He would report to them the crimes from the previous week and the outcome of each case. In any week that the number of crimes increased, he was authorized to double the force from twenty-five to fifty, and then to one hundred if necessary.

Within three months, crime in the West End stopped. And I mean stopped.

Within six months, retail sales returned to previous totals, and new merchants started coming back.

In this case, **the purpose was to restore the West End to a vibrant entertainment district.**

AH HA! It's not that complicated, just have breakfast every Tuesday

Surprise! Sports is Big Business

Economic development is not just corporate relocations or public safety. It's also creating excitement, crowds, and joy.

By February 1992, I knew that, but with the urgent problems confronting me every day, I hadn't started on sports.

I had promised a four-day ski vacation with my daughter, Allison. I didn't have time, nor could I afford it. But a promise is a promise.

We took the overnight bus to Taos over the Presidents' Day holiday.

Upon my return, a little groggy, I discovered eight of the major sports reporters in Dallas in my conference room. I had never met any of them. They were icons.

Dave Smith, sports editor of *The Dallas Morning News*, started bluntly: "Mayor, we've never talked to a politician before. We're sports guys. But we've heard some strange rumors. People are whispering that you think of sports as economic development. That is so unlike Dallas. Is that true?"

"Well, as a matter of fact, yes. I've not had time to start, but I plan to bring hockey, soccer, car races, and a lot more to Dallas. Nothing is ready yet, but we'll get started soon."

"Does that include a new NBA arena?"

"Yes, of course."

"And a National Hockey League team?"

"Also, of course. That's how we pay for the arena."

I think I went into some details of what I had in mind and the economic impact.

Dave Smith closed the meeting by saying, "We're with you, Mayor, but you're crazy. You'll never get this done. Not in Dallas."

The following week, I met with the head of the Dallas Sports Commission and asked for a detailed plan for recruiting an NHL team to Dallas. A week after receiving the report, Norm Green, owner of the NHL's Minnesota North Stars, called from his plane on the way to Palm Springs to ask if we wanted an NHL team in Dallas. I quickly flipped to the Minnesota tab in the Sports Commission's plan and saw why he was calling. Trouble in his home city.

When I said, "Come to Dallas and we will make it happen," I actually heard him say, "Pilot, turn left, we are going to Dallas." We had lunch the next day, joined by Roger Staubach, for heft, and we penciled out a deal.

And six weeks later, we had an NHL team. Followed by the Big 12 Headquarters, an annual Grand Prix race in downtown, the World Cup Semi-Finals and a Broadcast Center, and a rejuvenated Christmas Cotton Bowl Parade. Four years later, after I had left City Hall, we had a new NBA and NHL arena.

The purpose was straightforward: attract big sports to Dallas.

AH HA! **You've got to know what you want, and then go get it.**

When in Doubt, Change the Light Bulbs

More about downtown.

I didn't notice this in my first year. But by December of year two, I started to hear comments about downtown being dark and scary after 5:00 p.m. or so. As in, "I don't go downtown after 5:00 p.m., it's just so dark and dreary. I go to NorthPark or the Galleria. It's lit up like a Christmas tree."

I opened my eyes, and sure enough, downtown was dark and really uninviting.

I went to the City Manager. "What would it take to double the lighting in downtown Dallas?" She asked Public Works, and they came back with a $35 million estimate.

Whew. That wouldn't work, but we had to do something.

I asked Erle Nye, the president of Texas Utilities, to have breakfast with me. Usual spot, the Stoneleigh Hotel.

"Erle, downtown is way too dark. The City Manager tells me it would cost $35 million to double the number of light poles. Can you come up with a better solution, or at least split the cost with us? After all, you sell the electricity."

"I don't know, Mayor, but I'll find out. Breakfast next week?"

The next week, we sat down. I was anxious.

Erle leaned across the table and almost whispered, "Mayor, I have an answer, but I won't tell you unless you promise to never tell anyone what we are going to do. Promise? Because if people find out we had the wrong light bulbs, we would be laughed out of town."

Confused, I mumbled, "I promise."

"All we have to do is change the light bulbs to high-intensity bulbs. And we can pay for it with the electricity we save in one year."

Huh? I was stunned. "Well, that's it? That's all you have to do?"

"Now, Mayor, you promised."

He started changing the light bulbs that week, and before the winter was out, people started saying, "You know, Mayor, downtown Dallas looks so much brighter, just like NorthPark."

"Did you do something to make it brighter?"

My purpose was simple: turn on the lights in downtown. But I did not know the solution would be so simple.

But I kept my promise and never told how it was done.

Until now.

_AH HA!_ Just change the light bulbs.

Message to the Gangs: Stop the Shooting

Back to crime.

In the fall of my second year, KRLD Radio reported a drive-by shooting over the weekend that killed two people. When I got to the office, I asked the City Manager what happened.

She matter-of-factly said, "It was a drive-by, random, so there's nothing the police can do."

That bothered me, but I accepted the explanation. Wrong.

The following weekend, there was another drive-by, with another fatality. And the following weekend, another.

I saw a pattern, so I insisted on a briefing. Same answer. I asked the police to think about it.

And on the fourth weekend, another drive-by. This time, killing a six-year-old. I was furious.

When I arrived at my office, my staff later told me they had never seen me so angry.

Chief Rathburn and two deputy chiefs came to my office.

"Do you know who's doing the killing?"

"Yes, it's two teenage gangs having a war."

"How many gang members altogether?"

"Seventy-five."

Glaring, I asked, "So seventy-five suspects. Do you know their names? Their home addresses?" Of course they did.

"How many cops you got?"

"Three thousand."

Connect the dots.

"Spend the rest of the day and come up with a plan by 5:00 p.m."

The next day, the Chief announced that two patrol officers would follow each gang member wherever they went. Stick like glue.

Called "Zero Tolerance" in cop parlance. Any infraction—running a stop sign, two miles over the speed limit, spitting on the sidewalk—and gang members were arrested and booked. Their cars were impounded and held for a month.

My role was to get the most visible, respected Hispanic civil rights activist (these were Hispanic gangs) to announce the plan. Local icon Adelfa Callejo came through like a champ. I also asked Chief Juvenile Judge Hal Gaither to incarcerate arrested gang members for at least thirty days, and to state in open court that he was doing so because of the drive-by killings.

Now here's the secret sauce: every gang member was told directly by a uniformed officer, "We will stop following you when you quit the gang. And don't lie, because we'll know."

The two gangs were down to forty-two members within two weeks, and the police solved the murders.

And no more drive-by shootings. None. Not one.

My purpose was clear: stop the drive-by shootings.

AH HA! **You can be in a gang, but you can't shoot people.**

19 Mortgages for 235,000 Population

Returning to the economy.

I regret to say Dallas was still highly segregated in 1991, both by race and by economic class. I heard over and over, "There are no major banks in my part of town." Actually, there was one branch, Bank of America, that had opened six months earlier.

One-fourth of the city, about 235,000 people, was bordered by the Trinity River and I-30. Often called "the Southern Sector."

The biggest problem was the difficulty of getting mortgages. Hard to qualify and more expensive. And no local bank to apply to.

In December 1991 (yes, I jammed a lot of stuff into that first month), I asked the six largest home lenders in Dallas to meet for breakfast. Only Countrywide did not attend.

They knew there was a problem, but had no reason to do anything about it. I gave them a reason.

"Let's first scope the size of the problem. Meet me here in the first week of January and tell me how many mortgages you made in the Southern Sector in 1991."

Two weeks later, the answer: "Mayor, we are very, very embarrassed. It's far, far worse than we thought."

"How many?"

"Nineteen."

I was stunned. In fairness, so were the bankers.

"I'm sure you have an idea of how to fix this. After all, making loans is what you do. So, I'm going to leave you here for your first planning meeting. We can meet every ninety days for a progress report. And one year from today, right here, we will have breakfast again for you to report."

One year later, these five banks had changed their systems and issued over one thousand mortgages in the Southern Sector. Nineteen to one thousand. And these were good mortgages, meeting all underwriting standards.

I invited them to the next city council public session to receive public recognition. And, of course, it got better from there.

By the end of my term, there were five major bank branches in the Southern Sector, and home mortgages were readily available.

The purpose was straightforward: ensure that mortgages were readily available in all parts of Dallas.

AH HA! Sometimes it's just recognizing the problem.

Workforce Council: Read the Law

Sometimes the underlying problem is hubris.

Under the Job Training Partnership Act, which I had helped to reauthorize, Dallas received about five million dollars a year in job training funds. A little-known provision in federal law stated that the funds were allocated by the mayor unilaterally. It was designed for strong-mayor cities, true, but that was the law.

I knew Dallas' Private Industry Council (PIC) was woefully inadequate by state and national standards. Dallas was ranked last out of thirty-four PICs in Texas. But the Dallas PIC was quite powerful, with the Chairman being one of the former mayor's best friends.

So, I asked for a meeting with the chairman and president. I planned to offer to help them improve. Just the three of us. To my surprise, they presented a PowerPoint extolling their "success." All vague headlines, no specifics, and no identifiable results.

Stunned, I asked, "How many unemployed workers did you retrain last year? How many got jobs? With how many employers?" They didn't know.

"Okay," I said. "How can I help?"

"We don't need your help because we are already one of the best PICs in Texas, if not the nation. There are no improvements to be made. And further, you and the City have nothing to do with it. We report to the Department of Labor."

Realizing this was hopeless, I asked if we could meet again in one week, after I had digested their PowerPoint.

Reluctantly, they agreed.

I went back to City Hall to confirm that I did, in fact, have the unilateral authority to direct the funds to another agency.

The next week, I brought an assistant city attorney (the city attorney wanted no part of this). I showed them the appropriate section of the law and a letter notifying them that I would withdraw their funding in six months, absent significant improvements to my satisfaction. The assistant city attorney backed me up.

I asked for monthly reports detailing the number of unemployed workers they had trained and placed in jobs.

Within six months, they had improved. Not perfect, but enough to keep their funding.

And over time, tens of thousands of unemployed Dallas workers got training and full employment.

And that was the entire purpose.

AH HA! **Sometimes you just have to get their attention.**

And One More Jobs Moment

My first summer as mayor, I asked if we had a summer jobs program. Yes, I was told, so I took it off my "to-do" list. Wrong.

It turned out to be a Department of Labor grant made directly to the City of Dallas. The goal was to hire low-income teenagers for the summer. They were paid, but they didn't have to work.

All summer, I saw groups of teenagers hanging out around City Hall. I mean, literally hanging out.

I was told the City didn't have any jobs for them and didn't have the will or means to train them. As long as they showed up, they got paid.

I objected, but I couldn't make the Park Department get them to weed gardens or mow lawns.

The biggest problem was that we were teaching these teens the wrong lesson: that you didn't have to actually work to get paid. We may have ruined them for life.

The following November, I called Ben Casey, head of the Dallas YMCA, and asked him to design, fund, and operate a respectable summer jobs program. He agreed.

The following May, we rolled it out. He was even nice enough to call it "The Mayor's Summer Jobs Program."

Ben hired seasoned job counselors.

Every teen was guaranteed a job, on the condition that they showed up for interviews until they were hired. They actually told the teens, "The mayor guarantees you a job, as long as you show up for the interviews."

Nice touch.

After each interview, when a teen was not hired, the employer had to call the job counselor to explain why not. "Shoes untied, late for the interview, bad breath, no eye contact," and so on.

The job counselor then called the teen in to explain why they were denied, in a gentle yet specific way. It usually took two, three, or four interviews before the teen self-corrected.

Five thousand mostly low-income teenagers got real jobs, with real pay, real employers, and real work. Many were offered college scholarships and full-time jobs after graduation by their summer employers.

One of the more gratifying things I did as mayor. Thank you, Ben Casey and the Dallas YMCA.

A side note: The following summer, we added a program for rising ninth graders at Madison and Pinkston, the lowest-income schools in Dallas. We offered life skills—how to get and hold a job, shake hands and make eye contact, show up on time, avoid the gangs, study skills, and even how and why to avoid pregnancies. We called it "Summer of Choice."

At the closing awards banquet in August, a young, tough-looking kid approached me. "Mayor, I want to shake your hand. You saved my life."

"Huh? How did I do that?" I asked.

"In May, me and my buddies were planning to join the gangs. My girlfriend convinced me to try this for the summer.

"My three best friends joined a gang. Today, one is in prison, one is dead, and one is in a wheelchair. I figure I'd be the dead one."

I admit I choked up. It doesn't get any better than that.

On the surface, the purpose was jobs for five thousand teenagers. **But the real purpose was to show teenagers how to find a job, do the job, and keep the job.**

***AH HA!* Real jobs and real work change real lives.**

Supermarkets!

During my campaign for mayor, and indeed during my days on the city council, one of the most common complaints from the southern sector (the poor part of town) was the lack of first-class supermarkets. I mean none. And people knew what they were talking about.

Supermarkets in North Dallas were 50,000 square feet, light and airy, with fresh produce, well-lighted parking lots, and a healthy variety of food. The southern sector stores were old, a maximum of 30,000 square feet, with wilted produce, dark aisles, and often dangerous parking lots.

I went to the supermarket executives informally, and they all said, "Mind your own business, Mayor. Our grocery stores in low-income neighborhoods are just fine. People should stop complaining."

I learned that Fiesta Mart in Houston wanted to move to Dallas but hadn't gained any traction at Dallas City Hall.

So I made an appointment with Fiesta Mart in Houston, bringing the aforementioned Rick Douglas and City staff with me.

"Whatever you need to come to Dallas in the southern sector, you've got." We threw everything we had at them, including new streetlights and the city street that was in their way.

We put it on the council agenda, and it passed with the usual four dissenting votes.

Fiesta Mart opened a new, modern, well-lit 55,000-square-foot supermarket a block off Jefferson in the heart of Oak Cliff and announced two more. The first store was so popular that customers had to take a number to get in for the first couple of weeks.

The Dallas supermarket executives were furious. They came to see me to demand why I had given incentives to a Houston competitor.

I listened, reminded them I had asked them first, and then told them they could each have a Fiesta Mart-type deal if they built in low-income areas.

Kroger was the first, but they all eventually did.

Purpose, straightforward: quality and modern supermarkets in all parts of town.

***AH HA!* Somebody has to go first.**

Permanent Grass Field

During my campaign, I became aware that the City was submitting an active and energetic bid for some of the regional games of the World Cup. Good news, with hundreds of thousands of out-of-town visitors for each game.

So I joined the bandwagon.

It turned out that election day was the same day the Chairman of the Site Selection Committee came to town. I spent four hours with him and got an earful. He was angry.

By way of saying hello, he barked, "Let me tell you, Mr. Mayor, exactly why Dallas will get NO GAMES! NO GAMES!" Never mind that I hadn't even been elected yet.

Why was he so adamant? He told me explicitly, "Dallas is not complying with the terms of the bid in so many ways. You are off the list!"

He had specifics: no permanent grass field, the press box and VIP suites not even planned, and much more.

"You have ninety days to get your bid in compliance, or don't waste the postage."

I figured out the problem was good old familiar Dallas hubris. "We are Dallas, and we don't have to do those things."

I intervened, and things got back on track.

But the biggest issue remained: a permanent grass field at the Cotton Bowl. The Cotton Bowl had astroturf for thirty years. It was cheaper to maintain, but it was hard on athletes' knees and ankles, and totally unsuitable for soccer.

In early February, the City Manager invited me to a meeting to select the seats for the Cotton Bowl. There were six or seven city and park officials in the room.

Then I asked innocently, "Are we good with the permanent grass field?"

The answer blew me away. "Oh no, the Park Board can't afford the maintenance. So we will tear it out when the World Cup leaves town."

I calmly stated, "No. The grass is to be permanent. That's the bid requirement."

The First Assistant Manager, John Ware, was presenting. A real tough cookie.

"Mayor, do you have the authority to order a grass field?"

"John, do you or anyone in this room think I don't?"

No one spoke. After a long silence, John said, "Okay, permanent grass field it is."

But the grass field was not the purpose.

The purpose was to secure the World Cup for Dallas.

AH HA! Meet the specs, or don't bother to bid

Ann Richards: NAFTA, Target, Countrywide

Ann Richards was elected governor in 1990. She was liberal as hell, but charming, witty, and she tried to avoid a fight when she could.

She and I hit it off at once. What we had in common was a focus on jobs and economic development. Texas wasn't doing that great, and Dallas was in the tank.

The first big issue was NAFTA. A major economic deal for Dallas and Texas. It had stalled in Congress because of President Clinton's unwillingness to go to bat for it.

I heard NAFTA was in trouble, and why, from friends in Washington. I immediately called the governor and told her Bill Clinton was the problem.

"That sonofabitch! I'll take care of it."

An hour later, she called back to say, "It's taken care of." That afternoon, I was invited by the White House to join Ann Richards and two hundred other big shots in the East Room of the White House, invited by Bill Clinton himself. NAFTA passed within sixty days.

From global to local: two years later, I learned the Texas Highway Department was denying a left-hand turn on Loop 12 that would allow Target to build a store—the second Target store in the central city in the nation. No turn lane, no Target. A big deal.

I called the governor's office about 3:00 p.m. and asked that she call me. She called that night at 10:15 p.m. I was nodding off in bed.

"What's wrong?" I asked her. She instantly said, "That sonofabitch. Here's the direct phone number of the head of the Highway Department. Call him at 8:06 a.m., so I can chew him out first. He'll say yes."

I did, and he did. He also asked me to call him directly next time, rather than the governor.

Fast forward to early 1995. I asked Ron Kirk, Texas Secretary of State, to run and succeed me as mayor. Ron and I had been friends since my days on Capitol Hill, when he was an assistant city attorney. He would be the first African American to be mayor of Dallas—or indeed, even to be a credible candidate. He said no.

I called the governor. "That sonofabitch!" (Seems to be a common refrain.) "He will call you to say yes tomorrow afternoon by 3:00 p.m."

She invited Kirk to lunch in her office and wouldn't let him leave. He later claimed she posted a State Trooper, until he called me and said yes, 3:00 p.m. on the dot. He later told me it was the worst ass-whipping he had ever had. And Kirk was a great mayor.

She also called CEOs who were considering relocations to Dallas. She never asked for anything in return.

My purpose was neither to be friend nor adversary with Ann Richards. It was to harness the power of the governor for the public good.

AH HA! **You just have to know who to call.**

Shirts Off

One of the few "get away from it all" things I could do as mayor was go to a Rangers baseball game. Nine innings of chilling out with baseball talk and a couple of beers. I don't think I was ever recognized, or at least no one ever said, "Hello, Mayor."

I went to six or eight games a year, usually with my best friend, Jim Oberwetter. Sometimes Wick.

One afternoon game at Rangers Stadium, which was notoriously like a sun lamp in a sauna, we were in the sun, and it was hot. By the sixth inning, Jim and I took off our shirts, like half the men in the stadium.

The Rangers broadcaster was Norm Hitzges, a friend of ours, but this was too good to pass up.

Between innings, the TV camera was scanning the crowd, and Norm was laughing about how hot it was. Suddenly, he shouted on the air, "Stop! Is that the Mayor? With his shirt off and a beer in his hand?!"

He had a great time the rest of the game, bringing the camera back on yours truly.

Jim and I were unaware of the drama. When I walked in the front door, Gail handed me the phone. "It's your mother calling from Lone Star, and you are in trouble."

Innocently, I picked up the phone. "Yes, Ma'am." And that was all I was allowed to say.

"Son, what do you mean by taking off your shirt in public? The preacher called, and he is embarrassed, and I am embarrassed, and now I can't go to Walmart tomorrow because everyone in Lone Star knows!"

"Uh, but it was hot, it was baseball, I mean… Yes, Ma'am. Please apologize to the preacher for me. It will never happen again."

And it didn't.

My purpose was to make my mother proud.

AH HA! **Never take your shirt off in public. Your Mother is always watching.**

Katy Trail, Train to DFW, Cowboy Art, and Survivors Park

When I arrived as mayor, I stumbled over multiple worthy projects that had never proceeded. Never turned down exactly, just never authorized.

The reason was the aforementioned city council dysfunction. No one wanted to bring up something that someone would object to.

Survivors Park. I got a call from Richard Bloch of Kansas City. He was building and paying for small meditative parks all over the country. No cost to the city. Dedicated to cancer survivors. He had done twenty-five all over the country, and only Dallas had said no.

It turned out the Dallas Park Board had decided that if you did it for one disease, you'd have to do it for every disease. (They were thinking AIDS.)

I called Lois Finkelman, the president of the Park Board, and suggested they stop being afraid and get this done. She agreed, and Survivors Park is in downtown Dallas today. Not an ounce of controversy.

Katy Trail. Twelve years earlier, Katy Railroad had donated a five-mile right of way to the City from downtown to Mockingbird. Nothing had been done.

Why, I asked Lois. "Because somebody might object to joggers running past their neighborhoods."

Lois called a couple of public hearings. No one objected except four council members. The twelve-foot-wide bike path and companion eight-foot-wide soft-surface jogging path today carry hundreds of thousands of hikers, joggers, and bikers every year. It is one of the most popular amenities in Dallas.

Train to DFW Airport. This was another railroad right of way, donated to Dallas and Fort Worth by another railroad ten years earlier. Nothing had been started.

I asked the head of DFW Airport why. The answer: "We can't have Dallas build their connection (downtown to Terminal A) until Fort Worth is ready to build theirs."

Gag me with a spoon. I didn't mince words. I put it on the agenda to let both cities build their portion. Starting now.

Today, downtown to DFW via train is fifty minutes for six dollars. And Fort Worth built theirs as well.

Outdoor Longhorn Sculpture. Two benefactors who loved western art offered to donate a life-size sculpture of eighteen longhorns and three cowboys at the entrance to the Convention Center.

Wails of objection from the City Hall Public Arts Committee had killed the project. "Dallas is not Cowtown! It's bad art." It was actually good art, but more importantly, it was a tourist attraction.

Again, I called for a public hearing. Let everyone be heard, and then vote. Same four "no" votes, and today the Longhorns are a popular tourist destination.

In all these cases, **I identified the purpose and didn't get distracted by the noise.**

AH HA! **Have a public hearing, listen, and then vote.**

Convention Center Mural

Speaking of public art, a far more distressing incident happened in the fall of 1992. As you might have deduced by now, I did not have an especially good relationship with the City Manager I inherited.

This one I was able to solve quietly.

Robert Decherd, chairman, president, and CEO of Belo Corporation, which owned *The Dallas Morning News*, made an appointment to see me alone one afternoon. He didn't bring staff, and neither did I. Clearly, this was a big deal.

He got right to the point. "Mayor, it has come to my attention that the City's Public Arts Committee has approved a massive one-hundred-foot wall mural at the entrance to the new addition to the Convention Center."

Okay.

"The mural is described as the real history of Dallas, depicted in graphic display. It includes the Kennedy assassination, the murder of twelve-year-old Santos Rodriguez by a Dallas police officer, the deadly tornado of 1957, the lynching of an African American at Main and Akard, and half a dozen more. I can sit on this story for about a week, if you can get it stopped."

Holy sh*t! I could stop it, of course, but if I did so publicly, Dallas would still be mightily embarrassed.

"Robert, I will get this stopped quietly, I hope. I will call you by 5:00 p.m. Friday."

I asked the City Manager to come see me. Frankly, I assumed she didn't know anything about it, so she could quash it quietly.

Not so lucky. She told me she knew about it but couldn't stop it because the Dallas Arts Committee could not be overridden. Are you kidding? She was adamant.

I realized this was not a time to negotiate or debate. I played the big card.

"I understand what you are saying. Here's what I'm going to do. If you haven't killed this quietly by 5:00 p.m. Friday, I will call the City Secretary and place it on next Wednesday's agenda: 'Consideration of public art at the Convention Center.'

"I won't be embarrassed, but the City will, and you will."

She glared.

She called at 4:45 p.m. on Friday. "I killed it. I don't want to ever hear a word about this."

I called Decherd. Whew. Dodged that bullet.

And in case you wonder what she was trying to accomplish, I have no idea.

My purpose was to preserve Dallas' honor and reputation.

AH HA! Some things don't make sense.

Dallas' First Charter School

I had long been a fan of Dallas Can Academy, a non-profit school of about 500 high school dropouts. They had a 92 percent success rate. Success was defined as not only graduation but employment and enrollment in post-secondary education.

A 92 percent success rate with a population of 100 percent dropouts.

One day, I called Grant East, the founder and CEO, to ask if he could expand it, as Dallas had a lot more dropouts than 500.

"Sure, it's just money. All our funds come from charitable contributions. Costs about $1,500 per student."

DISD was receiving $4,600 a year from the state per student. But they lost $4,600 when a student dropped out.

This should be easy. Wrong.

I called Sandy Kress, the president of the School Board, and a friend. "How about enrolling the dropouts, receiving $4,600, you keep $1,600 and send $3,000 to Dallas Can to educate them? Only pay for the ones who graduate. Everybody wins."

Sandy said yes, of course, and turned it over to Superintendent Chad Wolery, who said yes but meant no. He would prepare the contracts.

I called every two weeks for three months, but couldn't get a clear answer. I even offered $3,000 to DISD and $1,600 to Dallas Can.

Finally, I realized I was being played.

"Chad, if you don't send me a contract by Friday, I will call my friend George W. Bush and make Dallas Can a charter school. Texas will pay Dallas Can the entire $4,600."

On Friday, I did, and we had the charter within a week. Dallas Can doubled its enrollment in one year and is today on multiple campuses with over 5,000 students.

A coda: Governor Bush came to speak to about 300 students a couple of months later. The students knew the deal and gave him a standing ovation on arrival and exit.

GWB took questions. One young guy, tough-looking, asked if he could come forward and shake Bush's hand. Security looked really nervous.

"No, but you can give me a big old man hug."

The hug lasted thirty seconds. Not a dry eye in the house.

Purpose: to recover thousands of high school dropouts and lead them to productive lives.

AH HA! Why is it so hard to do the right thing?

Homeless? Do You Want a Job, An Apartment, Food, or Anything Else?

Like most cities, Dallas had a homeless problem. Not as big a problem in the early 1990s as it later became, but still a nagging problem with no apparent solution.

A side note: the problems of homeless individuals generally include more than a shortage of housing. The problems are multifaceted and interconnected: jobs, medication, substance abuse, mental illness, and sometimes just getting off track. I am glad to say Dallas is now one of the cities making progress on those root causes, but that was not the case in 1992.

We had an immediate problem: large encampments of the homeless under the freeway overpasses. They were lighting campfires to cook and keep warm.

So what was the problem? TxDOT, the Texas Highway Department, sent us a notice that the fires under the overpasses were weakening them to the point that the elevated freeways were at risk of collapsing. YEEOW!

True? I don't know. But it's sure not something I was willing to risk. Plus, TxDOT said they would order our freeways closed if we couldn't get it stopped.

Close the freeways? Now that's a problem.

The council agreed and passed an ordinance banning camping under the freeways. Note, we didn't wait to try to solve every problem for the homeless population, only that you can't camp under the freeways.

Immediate outcries. Headlines and 6 p.m. news every night.

An activist for the homeless named John Fullenwider demanded that I meet with the homeless personally. Happy to. Tell me when.

Rather than make an appointment, he planned a surprise visit to my office. Of course, I got wind of his "surprise." (There are no secrets if you know where to listen.)

I was prepared. Fullenwider and a dozen homeless people came to the back door, and I invited them into my conference room. TV cameras were there to record the "confrontation."

As I expected, the homeless individuals were courteous and just wanted to be heard. So I listened, on camera, and they cited a multitude of problems: no jobs, no place to live, no access to medicine, no food. I took notes for about thirty minutes.

Then I said I did understand and wanted to help.

"I'm glad you came. In my office are several people from various agencies who can help. So, who would like an apartment, rent-free, so you can get on your feet?" No takers.

"Okay, how about a job? It's minimum wage, but you can start tomorrow. Health clinic? Food pantry?" No takers. They just wanted to camp under the bridge.

I asked the social workers to come in so all could see they were real.

I wished them well and told them my offer to help stands. All they had to do was call me. (Here's my card.) But they could no longer camp under the freeway.

We all shook hands, and I wished them well. Some thanked me.

Fullenwider glared.

My purpose was to help the homeless, but not allow them to live under the freeway.

_AH HA!_ I'll help, but you can't live under the freeway.

Museums For Everybody, If You're White

Back in 1979, when I was on the council, we passed a $400 million bond issue for the large arts institutions. An Arts District to house museums, concert halls, theaters, and opera. "Large" means mostly White patrons.

About five years later, the council passed more bonds for the Meyerson Symphony Hall. Political problem: the increasingly empowered African American community objected, "What's in it for us?"

So the council responded with $1.2 million to build an African American Museum of Art and Culture. They even designed the building. But they only partially funded it. The balance was to come from private donations.

Fast forward to 1992. The museum had developed a striking new design: large, full of light, with a dome. Price tag: $7 million. Curtis Meadows of the Meadows Foundation was the only, repeat only, major arts donor who was willing to help. He came to see me with Harry Robinson, Chair of the African American Museum. I didn't know Curtis, but Harry was a longtime friend. He controlled the core collections and had been working on this for twenty years.

"Bottom line is, Mayor, we cannot raise the $6 million in private money. Been trying for five years and got closed doors. Tried every major arts donor in Dallas."

Now, in context, the Symphony Hall price tag was $84 million, half from donors. The Art Museum had recently raised $27 million for an addition. Seven million for an African American museum seemed, well, paltry.

So Curtis went on, "But we have a solution. We have redesigned to reduce the size by seventy-five percent, shrinking the building from four great halls with a dome to one warehouse. And Harry is okay with it."

Seventy-five percent! From four halls to one?

I was apoplectic. "Harry may be okay with this, but I'm not. We will build the original design. You set up the calls with every prospect, in Dallas and nationally, and I will ask them myself. Start with the donors to the Art Museum and Symphony Hall. And the City will find extra money."

After that, a lot of people got involved in raising the funds. While I made a few calls, I didn't have to do much. Former mayor Annette Strauss was especially helpful and led the groundbreaking. And Harry solicited 50,000 small donors

It took six months to raise the money and a year to construct.

The grand opening was a joyous, festive occasion. I recall sitting next to Congresswoman Eddie Bernice Johnson. She was crying. "Steve, I never, never thought this could happen in Dallas."

My purpose was to get a first-class African American Museum built. Full stop.

AH HA! **If the White folks get a museum, so should everybody else.**

Never Seen So Many White People in One Place

It got worse.

Shortly after Harry and Curtis came to see me, the president of the Dallas Theater Center invited Gail and me to the opening night of *The Front Page.*

In context, the City of Dallas owns the theater itself and provides about twenty-five percent of the operating costs. And I was still a little sensitive.

The cast of about twenty-five was, how can I say this, all White.

Gail, reading my mind, kept squeezing my arm as I seethed. She whispered, "Don't say it. Don't do it. You are a guest."

As the house lights went up for intermission, the president inquired casually, "Well, Mayor, what did you think?"

Gail again whispered, "Don't say it."

Eyes straight ahead, I quietly intoned, "Well, I must admit it's been a long time since I've seen so many White faces in one place."

Silence. Gulp. Uh oh.

"Well, Mayor, I mean, we couldn't find any qualified Black actors."

I guess it was the word "qualified" that got me.

Silence. Then I said, "Let me see if I understand you clearly. You couldn't find any Black actors in a city of one million? Next time, call me, and I will send you some names. Fully 'qualified.'"

The second half was really quiet.

But the good news is that the Dallas Theater Center integrated its casts after that. The bad news is that I wasn't invited back either.

My purpose was not to manage the Dallas Theater Center. But I was determined to stop the segregation at a city-owned facility.

***AH HA!* This one speaks for itself.**

A Story About Jimmy Carter and Haiti

In late September 1994, I attended a meeting in Washington, D.C., of the U.S. Conference of Mayors. I felt that having at least one Republican in the room might help balance the National League of Cities' strong left-leaning tendencies.

During a recess, a friend and former congressman, who had also served as mayor of Philadelphia, pulled me aside. "Steve, I have to tell someone this unbelievable story, and I can trust you." There is a certain bond among ex-Congressmen.

Haiti had been governed by a military tribunal headed by General Cedras. He had called elections but made it clear he would not abide by the results unless he was elected. He wasn't.

Mobs were roaming the streets, and President Bill Clinton decided to send in the Marines.

Former President Jimmy Carter flew to Washington and asked for a chance to "give peace a chance." President Clinton reluctantly agreed to send Carter, Colin Powell, and Howard Baker to Haiti to negotiate, but told them they had to be back in the U.S. within seventy-two hours.

At noon on the appointed day, they sat down with General Cedras to talk. And talk. And talk.

It was 7:00 p.m. and time to leave, but Jimmy Carter never left his chair. Colin Powell went to a private room to call the White House. Bill Gray was in charge of the Situation Room.

"General Powell, President Clinton orders you, Baker, and Carter to leave."

"Bill, President Carter will not leave."

8:00 p.m. 9:00 p.m. 10:00 p.m. Telephone call every fifteen minutes. "He won't leave."

At 11:30 p.m., President Carter, who had not left his chair since 5:00 p.m., leaned over and said, "General, I haven't been totally honest with you. At midnight, a pre-programmed cruise missile is coming down that chimney. I'm prepared to die. Are you?"

At 11:45 p.m., General Cedras announced publicly that he was accepting the election and turning Haiti over to the elected President Aristide.

Colin Powell called the White House.

I don't know if the missiles were really coming down the chimney, but it was a pretty effective statement.

President Carter's purpose was to stop a war and install the elected government in Haiti.

***AH HA!* Sometimes, if you give peace a chance, peace sometimes wins. At least for a while.**

The Dallas Plan: If You Don't Know Where You Are Going, How Will You Know When You Get There?

Toward the end of my term, I realized it was time to start a new chapter. Violent crime was declining, downtown was showing life, economic development was achieving results, and the council was functional.

So, as I always did, I went to the City Manager. "Let's build something."

Wake-up call: the Manager replied that the cupboard was bare. We did not have a single capital works project in the planning stages, much less one with bond funding. The city had been in "managed decline" for eight years.

Hmmmm. So I went to my friend, mentioned earlier, Robert Decherd. The *Dallas Morning News* had published an eight-week series entitled *Vision Dallas.* They laid out a vision of what Dallas could be if we got our act together.

"Robert, you had the vision. Now I'd like to appoint you to chair a special commission to convert your vision into a plan."

In the words of an '80s musical number, "you've got the right string, Baby, but the wrong yo-yo."

"I won't chair the commission, Mayor. After all, I am a newspaper publisher. But I know the man who will. Robert Hoffman."

Ah, Robert K. Hoffman, a true Renaissance man. Brilliant businessman and entrepreneur, young, energetic, and civic-minded. And for good measure, he was a friend of mine and of Wick Allison. Hell, he was even in our monthly poker group.

Decherd paid for the whole thing, so we didn't get stuck in the City Hall bureaucracy. But we housed The Dallas Plan office at City Hall, on the City Manager's floor. That gave us the best of both worlds: outside independence and inside access. Robert hired a brilliant urban planner from back east, Judith Kovisars. She kept me informed, but I did not direct the project.

Deanne Kissematakis, my amazing scheduler, named it "The Dallas Plan" on a callback message. She said it was because she didn't know what else to call it. The name stuck.

Robert and Judith started with the public. They held some thirty-five meetings across Dallas, asking citizens for their vision of what the city could become. Then came the most brilliant insight: instead of starting with what was wrong, they began with what was right, the major assets Dallas already had that could be leveraged to build the future.

I think the assets were downtown, residential neighborhoods, our sports teams, Love Field, the park system, the Trinity River, and the business community, or some combination of those.

Use our strengths to solve our weaknesses.

They went back to the public with their draft, listened again, and adjusted. The plan passed the council unanimously, then was converted to a bond issue that passed with 65 percent approval.

And Dallas was back in business.

The purpose was to articulate the city's mission clearly, and build capital assets to achieve it.

With urgency.

***AH HA!* If you can dream it, you can achieve it.**

The Icing on the Cake. Carpe Diem Again

After The Dallas Plan had been adopted, and on the very day it was on its way to the printers, a miracle happened.

James Shinn was head of the Dallas International Department at the time. Good guy and smart. He had been skiing in Europe for a month.

He burst into my office directly from the airport, out of breath and really excited.

"Mayor, I've got it, a revelation! I saw this myself in Europe, and it is transformational!"

He handed me a one-page memo entitled *"Carpe Diem!"* (Seems like I've heard that before.)

The idea was to use the asset of a freeway to also create an urban park—by depressing the freeway and building the park on top. Magic. You still get the traffic flow of the freeway, you get a connection between the two sides, and you get an urban park, all instead of an ugly barrier.

And Dallas had the perfect candidate: Woodall Rogers was an elevated freeway separating downtown from Uptown, creating blight on both sides.

Stunned, I said, "It's too late, Jim."

"It's never too late to do the right thing, Mayor. *Carpe diem.*"

So I called Robert Hoffman and Judith. Their response was, "It's a brilliant idea, I wish we had thought of it, but it's too late. And how would we pay for it?"

"It's never too late. Just stick it in under Transportation, or Parks, or Downtown, and when the time comes, someone else will figure out how to pay for it."

At the time, I did not realize that burying Woodall Rogers had long been a whispered dream. Since the 1960s, urban designer Vince Ponte and *Dallas News* architectural commentator David Dillon had mused about it, but it had always been dismissed as "dreaming."

Ten to fifteen years later, led by then-mayor Ron Kirk, mayor Laura Miller, and Dallas Chamber executive Jody Grant, Dallas tore down Woodall Rogers, buried it, and built an urban park with volleyball courts, running tracks, trees, retail, fountains, and more. Klyde Warren Park is regarded today as the number one urban amenity in Dallas. It transformed both Uptown and downtown.

Why Klyde Warren? Because Dallas was millions of dollars short of paying for the park, and a prominent Dallas businessman, Kelsey Warren, offered to make up the difference if they would name it for his son, Klyde. Maybe a slight violation of the official naming criteria, but where there's a will, there's a way.

I figured out the purpose here after the fact: to remove the barrier between two parts of the city so both could help the other prosper.

AH HA! Carpe diem.

BACK TO WASHINGTON

Four Years in the Wilderness

This is embarrassing to relate. In my entire life, I had never been without a clear set of goals and a path to achieve them: start a High School Republican Club, proceed to State Chairman, then to president of the Republican Men's Club, then start Meridian, then to city council, then to Congress, then to mayor, and then… then… then… fuzzy and almost drifting. I say almost because it's not as if I wasn't working long hours.

But I couldn't figure out my purpose. I considered and unwisely rejected several career options: an MBA at the University of Texas, executing my Buy-Sell Agreement at Meridian, buying an oil exploration company in West Texas, joining Bruce Ledbetter to start an airline, moving to Washington, lobbying in DC (ugh), asking Ray Hunt or other Dallas executives for a real job, joining the Governor Bush Administration, or doing M&A deals. I dabbled in representing a private water company to privatize municipal water supplies and made a few speeches around the country on behalf of the Labor Policy Association.

In the end, I joined a private equity firm to buy another plastics company like Meridian, this one in Phoenix. I worked my ass off, but discovered I didn't really know how to operate a company. Lost a million dollars, and my Meridian business partner, Jim Foxx, exercised his Buy-Sell Agreement on me. Can't say I blame him, but I was out. O.U.T.—*Out!*

That's when my sweet, discerning, clever, smarter-than-me wife, Gail, saved me. She threw me a lifeline at dinner one night.

"You've been doing a lot of business things. How do you think it's going?" she asked sweetly.

"Fine. I mean, *fine*! Why do you ask?" I glared.

Then she got really serious. "Because you are a pretty good businessman," she lied, "but you are a great politician. You are the best politician I have ever even heard of. Is there a way to make money in politics? I mean, honestly, of course."

After a sleepless night, the next morning I called several friends in Washington, including the aforementioned Becky Campoverde and Lisa Stoltenberg, and posed that question.

"Of course," they said. "A trade association CEO. You run your own shop, keep it ethical, report to an industry board of directors, engage in public policy, and the compensation for a small one is $500,000 plus, and for a large one, north of a million."

Huh? Why hadn't someone told me this?

It was July 1998. I called the major search firms the next day, landed on the short list three or four times, and secured the position of CEO at The Financial Services Roundtable by June 1999. It was one of the big ones.

My purpose was to find my place in Washington.

AH HA! When in doubt, ask your spouse.

You've Confused My Search Committee

Not that the search was easy. But it was something I understood, and I could use my assets: a positive Washington reputation, strategic management skills, a strong network of friends in D.C., an understanding of public policy, and a breadth of knowledge across most industries. For the headhunters, I was an attractive candidate, a former mayor and a respected former congressman. The headhunter would look good whether I was chosen or not.

I was even a finalist for the top trade association job in D.C., the U.S. Chamber of Commerce. The job went to Tom Donohue, as it should have. But the headhunter, Craig Fuller, paid me the ultimate compliment by saying I had made a great impression on the search committee. I think he said something like, "You have confused my search committee," which I took to mean they were impressed.

After that, I was on my game, working at it nearly every day, leaving nothing to chance, following every lead, learning the inside culture of each organization, using my D.C. connections, and building a team headed by Lisa McGreevey and Becky Campoverde to gather information. It was like running for Congress inside the Beltway. One caveat: I had to push hard but not appear pushy. Like a duck moving fast through the water, calm and unruffled on the surface but paddling like hell underneath.

I was also a finalist for the National Association of Home Builders, the Mortgage Bankers Association, and several others. In one case, a twenty-two-member search committee met in person and was deadlocked in a tie for eight hours.

In the end, I was selected by The Financial Services Roundtable, one hundred of the largest banks and financial services companies in America. It was perfect for me.

And Gail was thrilled. I choose to think she was proud of me. But it might have been the money.

My purpose was to advance good public policy and be well compensated for doing it.

***AH HA!* Search and you shall find.**

Read This and I'll Be Back

The Chairman of the Search Committee, which never actually met, was Bob Gillespie, CEO of Key Bank of Cleveland. The Roundtable was hierarchical; the Chairman called the shots and cleared everything with the members.

With one exception, I soon discovered: Richard Kovacevich, CEO of Wells Fargo. He was the "Godfather" who had created the vision for the new Roundtable, and for that matter, the new industry. Ultimately, the new CEO was his call.

Mr. Gillespie didn't want to make a mistake. The search took nine months, with one or two meetings or conference calls with individual CEOs every month. Mr. Gillespie kept the conversation moving along as he considered a dozen prospects, comparing them all with me.

Mr. Kovacevich was behind the scenes, expressing his doubts and questions to Mr. Gillespie. Meanwhile, I was doing my due diligence on the current Roundtable. Let's just say, it was a mess, but I understood how to fix it.

The big issue was financial services reform and modernization. The industry had tried to pass a bill for twenty years. Always close, but always defeated.

In December, Mr. Gillespie called to ask me to meet him in New York at the St. Regis, in the presidential suite. At the door, he asked me to wait while he escorted his wife to the waiting cars to go to the airport with her Christmas shopping.

Before he left, he handed me a ten-page document with a plan for passing modernization. "Read this."

When he returned, he asked, "What do you think?"

I replied, "What do you think?"

"It's pretty bad, isn't it?"

"Yes."

"What would you do?"

I outlined, on one page of a legal pad, how I would approach it, and then said matter-of-factly, "If you hire me, I will get the bill passed."

It took until June to get Mr. Kovacevich and the other CEOs on board, but that assertion was the winning formula. Self-confidence with a plan.

We passed modernization, known as Gramm-Leach-Bliley, by the following November. And that was my immediate purpose.

***AH HA!* Do your homework. Have a plan that you can explain on one page, and be confident.**

Creating a New Association From An Existing One

Back to Washington

In summary, the Roundtable was a mess:

- Membership was at fifty-six companies, losing an average of six every year.
- Staff had been without leadership for a year and a half, maybe longer.
- Staff were demoralized at best. On my first day, I showed up at 7:30 a.m. Staff members straggled in as I sat in the reception area and greeted each one with a handshake. I then conspicuously

wrote down their name and time of arrival. The last one arrived at 10:30 a.m.

- There was no clear mission. Several CEOs told me there were only two committees: the Golf Committee and the Tennis Committee. And they were thinking about getting rid of Tennis.

- Even the name "Financial Services Roundtable" had been adopted just thirty days earlier, after considerable debate. Mr. Gillespie told me, "We did the hard part. You take it from there."

- Membership criteria were indistinct, hoping to add insurance and securities firms to the old Bankers Roundtable, but with no plan to do so.

- Five existing trade associations were already in this space, all quite protective of their territory.

- Dues were insufficient to fund the overhead. We would be bankrupt in eighteen months.

I accepted the job on June 1, with June 7 as my first day. As Gail and I were driving to D.C. with my clothes in the back seat, Mr. Gillespie called to invite me to a conference call meeting of the Membership Committee on Thursday. I called in from Little Rock, Arkansas. The meeting of eleven CEOs was, at best, incoherent. It started with a blank piece of paper and ended with no coherent plan. The old adage came to mind: "A camel is a horse designed by committee."

I called Mr. Gillespie immediately after the call ended.

"Steve, what did you think?"

"Mr. Chairman, what did you think?"

"Pretty bad, huh?"

"Well, it's a start. Who kept the minutes?"

"Rich Whiting, the General Counsel." He became a great ally of mine.

"Would you ask him to sit on the minutes, and I'll take care of it when I get to Washington? I will bring you a membership plan in thirty days."

Relieved, the Chairman agreed. And I brought him a coherent plan in less than thirty days, which the Membership Committee adopted as their own. For his comfort, I brought his lead consultant from the fabled business consultant McKinsey and Company to present the plan.

Whew. Dodged the first bullet.

My purpose was to create a coherent plan for the Roundtable, and get it approved quickly.

AH HA! **Control the minutes.**

Getting Started

To my good fortune, my best friend, Wick Allison, had just published a book on the lessons of history. He sent me the chapter on Clovis of early France. The summary: learn an organization's culture and use that existing culture to accomplish your objectives.

The culture of my members was clear: CEOs call the shots, we have to modernize the regulatory system if we are to survive, take responsibility, and act fast.

First step: Share with the existing staff the mission as defined by the CEOs and the new name, an industry-wide trade association including all elements of financial services (banks, insurance, and securities).

Second step: The mission in Washington is to pass legislation on behalf of our members. Lisa Stoltenberg, mentioned in previous chapters, was my most powerful hire as head of Government Affairs.

Third step: Ensure every staff member has a clearly defined mission. Identify the keepers and replace the others with higher-potential personnel. Courteously and fairly, but within ninety days.

Fourth step: Actively listen to the fifty-six CEOs, starting with the thirty on the board of directors. It took me three months, mostly in person. The result: I learned a few things, of course, but more than that, it was about showing respect and building loyalty.

Fifth step: Create a functional membership system. As I said, I hired McKinsie for this, although it was my plan from the start. But McKinsey gave it legitimacy.

Sixth step: Present my credentials to the power players in Washington, including Capitol Hill, other trade associations (emphasizing "We are all in this together"), agencies, the financial press, and the bank lobbyists who worked for my members. I made sure Washington knew I had arrived. Aside: my first stop on the Hill was Barney Frank, by then the ranking Democrat on the Banking Committee. The word spread that I was truly bipartisan.

Seventh step: Push hard and fast for financial services modernization. After all, that was why I was hired.

Finally, and most importantly, light a fire. Our staff and much of the industry were quite complacent. The most common phrase I heard from industry lobbyists, said in jest but not really, was, "We can't pass this yet. Not everyone has put their kids through college." I created a sense of urgency, ruffling a lot of feathers.

In essence, I was setting the agenda and the pace for the entire industry.

My purpose was to create a powerful trade association to achieve public good.

AH HA! Start Fast and Set the Agenda.

Urgency: 4:00 p.m. Every Monday at My Table

As to modernization, I had two essential requirements: create a sense of urgency and establish a belief that it could be done. After all, this had been on the table for twenty years.

I started by inviting the bank lobbyists who had been working on this for decades to my conference room. I told them we could finally pass modernization and do it this year.

To put a little fear and motivation in their hearts, I told them their CEOs expected us to do so. And I was talking to those CEOs regularly. They did not work for me, but they knew I talked to their bosses.

Then I told them we would meet in my conference room every Monday at 4:00 p.m., a dead time on Capitol Hill. All were invited, but none were required to attend. The only condition was that anyone who made a "side deal" the previous week was required to report it to the group the following Monday. It was the individual carveouts, exceptions, and special agreements that had killed the bill in previous sessions. Anyone who could not comply should leave now.

One lobbyist for a large financial institution left the room and never came back. But the remaining twenty became a remarkably coherent, effective, unified, and growing group. Every Monday at 4:00 p.m.

The key vote in the House was the rule bringing the bill to the floor. Defeating the Rule was how modernization had been killed in previous sessions. At our 4:00 p.m. Monday meeting, we concluded we were eight votes behind. The collective knowledge of these lobbyists was powerful. We identified the ten truly undecided Members.

CEOs to the rescue. I put in calls to the CEOs whose banks were in the districts of those undecided Members. Two CEOs, from Bank One and First Virginia, called the undecided and delivered eight votes. The Rule in the House passed by a six-vote margin.

During that summer and fall, the bill went back and forth. Most industry observers still did not believe it was possible. In fact, it was not done until after midnight on the last night of the Conference Committee, with a face-to-face confrontation between Phil Gramm and Treasury Secretary Larry Summers.

The 4:00 p.m. Monday meeting achieved urgency and unity.

The iconic Richard Kovacevich pulled me aside privately during the next meeting of the CEOs, put his hand on my shoulder, looked me straight in the eye, and said, "You did what you said you would do. Much faster than I ever thought possible. I have no more doubts." Clearly, he had had some doubts about me, and this was his way of clearing the air.

And thus Gramm-Leach-Bliley was born.

The legislation I was hired to pass was done in six months. My reputation was secure in Washington and with my CEOs.

The purpose was to energize and unify the industry to pass this long-overdue bill.

AH HA! Urgency and teamwork

Over the Transom and The Loaded Gun

I had no illusion that just because I had put Gramm-Leach-Bliley (GLB) on a fast track, energized the bank lobbyists, and made believers of my CEOs, I was out of the woods.

I had stepped on some powerful toes: the CEOs of the five existing trade associations who had been comfortably in charge. Before the end of June, I had met face-to-face with the CEOs of the trades for securities, banks, life insurance, property insurance, mutual funds, and banks.

They all pledged cooperation and unity. They all lied. They all felt threatened. The powerful, 100-year-old American Bankers Association, with 6,000 members, was the worst.

I only had fifty-six bank members, but I had the big ones. I was under instructions to get along as well as I could. But get the damn bill passed.

The first indication of a real problem started in July. I started getting calls from bank CEOs who had been "visited" by a very powerful bank lawyer from Washington. Hired by the ABA. Yes, I know who it was, but I will not disclose, as he has never told me directly.

The story was always the same: "Bartlett is a disrupter. We all got along until he came. He is destroying our unity. Fire him."

My CEOs all told the lawyer, and me, they had hired me to be a disruptor, so keep it up.

Then, in late July, I was sitting in my morning bagel shop near my office. A guy came in wearing a trench coat with the collar pulled up and a hat pulled low. He handed me an envelope with a five-page memo, said, "You should see this. Don't say where you got it."

You can't make this stuff up. In Washington, it's called "over the transom."

A five-page plan from these five CEOs detailing how they would get rid of me. By name.

At Lisa's counsel (thank Gawd I had her around), I calmly called each one and said I knew they had nothing to do with this, but could they help me understand? They each pointed fingers at the other four.

Then, in August, they dropped the big one. A story appeared on the front page of *American Banker* describing the unrest I was causing. The only one quoted was LeeAnn Pusey, a friend of mine from Congressional days and COO of the property insurance group.

Modernization had been defeated every year because the industry was not unified. Each group was trying to get a special deal.

I put the newspaper in front of her and calmly asked her why she said these things. She replied, "Because that's what I believe."

"If a story like this ever appears again, let me describe what I believe." Then I laid it out in gruesome detail: the lavish expense accounts, long vacations, no presence on the Hill, Congressmen laughing at them behind their backs, lobbying for twenty years to put their children through college, lack of effort, lack of urgency, and lack of competence.

"I will say these things in *American Banker*, *The Washington Post*, *The New York Times*, to my CEOs, to your CEOs, and maybe even on TV news. I will make a new accusation every day until everyone's house burns down. And whether you are quoted again or not, I will come after you and your boss first, and then go after the others.

"And my CEOs will back me up."

It's called "pull out the loaded gun and point it."

Shocked, she said, "But those things are not true."

"Some are, but they all will be true after I say them."

Deep breath, then, "Steve, you have my word. This will never happen again."

And it didn't.

LeeAnn became a good friend, and I generally had a good relationship with the others.

My purpose, unfortunately, had to be to inflict pain so the industry could accomplish its mission. Hard way to do it, but the only way.

AH HA! **Sometimes you have to show them your loaded gun.**

One Hundred Members!

When I signed on, the Roundtable was down to fifty-six member companies and losing a net of six per year. When I presented Chairman Gillespie with my membership plan, I asked why he hadn't told me the Roundtable would be bankrupt in eighteen months.

"Because I knew you would figure it out."

We adopted a plan to open up the former Bankers Roundtable to securities, insurance, and other elements of the financial services industry.

We limited membership to one hundred. Members had to be large as measured by market cap, represented by their CEO, and attend the meetings. Up to five other executives from each company could also be members. Most considered it such an honor that they listed it on their official résumés.

Dues were tiered in groups of ten, with amounts assigned by tier rather than formula. That way, if we only had, say, eighty members, we would lose only the smallest dues tiers.

We also created a separate Government Affairs Council, with as many lobbyists, lawyers, or public affairs staff as a company wanted to send. The GAC (150 members strong) became a powerful force in Washington.

Our first meeting with non-bankers was at the Plaza Hotel in New York on November 30, 1999. That was the fifth Wednesday of the month. Most CEOs organize their schedules by week, and every other day of the month was filled with standard meetings, except the fifth weekday.

We invited twenty-two CEOs. All attended, and all except Goldman Sachs joined on the spot.

They were interested in only two things: would the CEOs be in charge, and could we pass legislation?

The first answer was obvious. The CEOs were in charge. Just look around the table.

Legislation was another matter. They had been burned before by empty promises. But we had already passed Gramm-Leach-Bliley, so I had some credibility. I gave them a list of five or six legislative priorities. They still weren't buying it.

So I asked, "Would increasing annual contributions to $5,000 and 401(k)s to $15,000 make a difference?" It had been $2,000 and $5,000 for twenty years.

Skeptical stares. "Well, sure, but you can't do that."

"How big a difference would that make to you?"

One CEO pulled out his pocket calculator and replied, "That would add a nickel to my quarterly earnings in the first year." FYI, that's a lot.

"If you gentlemen join us, you'll have that within two years."

They didn't believe me, but they decided to give it a shot.

After that, I went to the remaining CEOs in the industry one at a time, always bringing an existing member CEO with me. We hit one hundred by the following June.

Side note: the last one was GE Capital, at the time the fifth largest financial institution in our membership. When they agreed to join, we already had one hundred, which was the limit. I called my Chairman to ask what to do. He said, "Don't be stupid, we'll just have one hundred and one for a while."

Was my purpose one hundred members? Not really. It was to achieve a critical mass of the industry. And one hundred members was a good surrogate for that.

AH HA! **CEOs Rule. And all they want are results.**

Laura Lane: The Most Courageous Person I've Ever Met

Let me be clear, I've met courageous people: Mother Teresa, John McCain, Army Ranger Steve Spence, and Police Chief Bill Rathburn, to name a few.

But Laura Lane is in a class by herself.

I met Laura in the early 2000s when she was a policy professional in the D.C. office of Citigroup, specializing in international trade. The Citigroup office was well staffed with capable people, but Laura immediately, I mean instantly, caught my attention. She was very smart, had a command of the facts, made direct eye contact, went right to the point, and didn't waste time.

I decided to look her up and discovered Laura's role in the Rwandan Genocide.
She was a twenty-four-year-old junior foreign service officer at the U.S. Embassy in Kigali, Rwanda. It was her first overseas assignment, and no doubt she was the youngest on staff.

As the genocide began, she went to the streets to see for herself what was happening. She asked her Rwandan friends. It was mass murder, a genocide.

She returned to the Embassy and marched into the Ambassador's office. He said something to the effect of, "The official U.S. policy is that this is a civil war, and we don't get involved in civil wars."

Eyes ablaze, Laura declared, "This is a mass murder, with machetes, a genocide."

And in what could have been a career-ending move, she picked up the telephone on the Ambassador's desk, called the U.S. State Department, handed the phone to the Ambassador, and said, "Tell them it is a genocide."

Twenty-four-year-old Laura Lane then marched back to the street and began organizing car caravans for Rwandans under attack.

With only her diplomatic passport as "protection," she and her driver led hundreds to the Ugandan border, two hours away.

They were stopped at checkpoints each trip by the genocidaires armed with AK-47s, ordering her to turn back. She calmly showed her passport and kept driving.

At one checkpoint, she was stopped by a young teenager with an AK-47. He literally placed the gun to her forehead, shouting, "Turn around, or I will blow your head off." Laura never broke eye contact with the young man. She motioned to her driver and calmly but firmly said, "Drive on."

Laura Lane saved hundreds of Rwandans from certain slaughter, armed only with her courage. She is a true American hero.

She was soon ordered to evacuate, but returned with the first humanitarian envoy from the United States.

Laura Lane's purpose was to save lives, and she personally saved hundreds.

AH HA! **If you've got courage, you can do anything.**

9/11! Up Close and Personal

Without a doubt, every American knows exactly where they were when the planes flew into the Twin Towers and the Pentagon. Our lives and our place in the world changed forever.

I was meeting with a small breakfast group, listening to Senator Evan Bayh take questions on the issues of the day. His staff assistant interrupted him to say they had to leave.

"Ok, ok, I'll just take two more questions."

The staffer got right in his face and said, "No. We have to leave. Now."

I had never seen anything like that before.

When I got to the street, it was pandemonium. People were running in all directions.

I was able to reach my General Counsel, Rich Whiting, by cell phone before connections went down. Our offices were two blocks from the White House. I told him to get everyone out immediately, and I meant immediately. Take the stairs in case the elevators stopped. Get home as best they could.

I ran the four blocks to my office. All staff had left, thank goodness.

The phones were dead, but the internet still worked. So I spent the day in constant communication with my members all over the country. They were all fearful, of course, but relieved to hear from someone they knew, right from the epicenter.

I stayed all day, sending and receiving emails, giving up-to-the-minute and personal reports. Many later told me it was reassuring to hear from the Capitol that all was not lost.

Of course, Gail and my daughters were frantically demanding that I return home to safety. I ignored them because I had a job to do.

I left the office around 8:30 p.m., satisfied that I had done my duty. Outside, armored personnel carriers and soldiers with rifles stood on every corner. A Metro police officer was kind enough to give me an escort.

My members often traveled during the week, so many were stranded all over the country, far from their home offices. For the rest of the week, I stayed in communication with them, offering information on which highway routes were open and the latest word from Washington.

I got the last member out of their remote location at 3:00 PM on Friday. Jim Blanchard, CEO of Synovus, had been stuck in Omaha all week, and his home office in Columbus, Georgia, needed his presence. I called to tell him his plane was cleared to fly. He said thank you as he was running out the door.

My purpose that day was to reassure my 300 members that we would get through this. And I'm glad I stayed at my post to do my job.

***AH HA!* September 11, 2001, changed the world and our place in it forever.**

Burn the Boats: Committee Realignment

When Hernán Cortés invaded Mexico in 1519, he had six hundred soldiers. The Aztecs had an armed population of twenty-five million. After landing on the beach, Cortés burned his boats, making a statement to his troops that there would be no retreat. If you wanted to go home, you had to conquer Mexico.

By November of 2000, it was clear to me that we could never pass another piece of financial services legislation because jurisdiction was divided between two committees, Banking and Commerce. And Commerce was against everything we wanted to do. Everything.

I did not know of any historical precedent for realigning committees in the House. It was just never done because you stepped on too many fiefdoms.

At the same time, there was an unusual leadership contest. Marge Roukema had the seniority on Banking. Next in line, Richard Baker was conservative and quite well liked, but choosing Richard meant bypassing a woman, which was politically risky.

The Commerce side was the bigger challenge. Billy Tauzin had seniority in Congress but not in the GOP. He had switched parties to the GOP ten years earlier. Mike Oxley had the party seniority. Both had seniority, both were well-liked, and neither was backing down. The Republican Conference was headed for a fratricidal floor fight.

Lisa and I brainstormed a rather elegant but risky solution. Move Mike to the Banking Committee and make him Chairman. Make Tauzin Chair of Commerce. Change House Rules to send all financial services legislation to the newly named House Financial Services Committee.

Somebody had to put his head in the noose. That was me.

I briefed Mike on the plan. "You're crazy," he said, "but if you succeed, they'll call me Mr. Chairman. If you fail, I never knew you."

I drafted a two-page letter to Speaker Denny Hastert on the board of directors' letterhead. My chairman, Ed Rust, CEO of State Farm and Denny Hastert's congressman, was at the top of the letterhead. I signed it as the sole signatory. The other trades declined to sign.

Lisa delivered it personally (a kind of reverse "over the transom") and made sure it was sitting on the Speaker's desk when he came back from the House Floor. She called in a few favors.

An hour later, Denny summoned Mike.

"Did you know anything about this, Mike?"

"Uh, oh, well, kinda, I guess."

"Are you for it?"

"Yes, I am."

"Done. I think we've solved our Chairman problem. Tell Tauzin."

And from that point on, all financial services legislation has gone through the House Financial Services Committee.

If this gambit had failed, I would have had the biggest target on my back in Washington.

I kept my purpose: to create the conditions for good financial services legislation to become law. While risky, this was the only way to succeed.

AH HA! **You've got to take big chances to get big rewards.**

Post GLB: E-Sign, Class Action, $5K IRA, FCRA, and More

And we were off to the races. Hard to believe, but financial services legislation had been largely ignored for twenty years. The industry was fragmented; modernization had soaked up all the energy; the Commerce Committee didn't want any changes; the Banking Committee spent most of its time on politically rewarding housing issues; and banking lobbyists focused only on their individual companies.

But now the industry was united, the Commerce Committee was out of the way, the Senate was favorable, my CEOs were engaged, and company lobbyists had learned that unity was power. The Government Affairs Council was up to 150 members, meeting monthly for three to four hours at a time.

And hard to believe, but large banks and financial services were actually popular. (That changed dramatically during the Great Recession of 2007 to 2009.)

So, with CEO input and approval, we adopted an ambitious agenda:

$5,000 IRAs. More on that later.

Electronic Signature. Brought to us by Fidelity Investments with the support of the tech industry. Before this, you had to provide a physical signature for every transaction, which was becoming a paperwork nightmare and an open invitation to fraud. It took all year, but in the end, the Clinton Administration, and Gary Gensler specifically, took the lead.

I was the last phone call Gary made before recommending that President Clinton sign the bill. Today, we take for granted the ability to sign documents electronically.

Class Action Reform. Four "plaintiff friendly" counties in the U.S. received 70 percent of all class action lawsuits, all heard in state courts. One plaintiff claiming harm, usually solicited by the lawyer and paid maybe $1,000, multimillion-dollar payments to the lawyers, and the "class" often got a coupon and little or no cash. A true scam. The U.S. Chamber had been working on this for ten years. I literally sent several of my CEOs to Capitol Hill to meet with undecided senators. When we joined the fight with new energy, the bill finally passed, and interstate class action lawsuits were sent to federal courts for fair trials. The result: aggrieved parties could finally get justice in fair courts.

Fair Credit Reporting Act. This had been the foundation of the credit score system for twenty years, but its federal preemption was expiring. Without preemption, there would be no credit score system, and therefore, no credit. A lender in Texas or New York would have no way of knowing if a borrower had defaulted on loans in Ohio or California. Each borrower would have to be investigated individually in all fifty states. The public did not like credit scores, so it was an uphill battle. It took two years and a massive effort. The iconic Richard Kovacevich led the task force with ferocity.

From 2000 to 2008, we were on a roll.

Purpose: to pass good legislation, not just talk about it.

_AH HA!_ Strike while the iron is hot.

Operation Hope

CEOs Rule. Richard Kovacevich of Wells Fargo was the permanent driving force as Chairman of the Nominating Committee, which nominated the next year's Chairman and Board. Chairmen included Bob Gillespie of Key Bank, Gene Miller of Comerica, Ed Rust of State Farm, Don Shepard of Aegon, Richard Davis of U.S. Bank, John Stumpf of Wells Fargo, Bud Baker of Wachovia, Jim Blanchard of Synovus, Jim Rohr of PNC, Tom Wilson of Allstate, Tom James of Raymond James, Ken Thompson of Wachovia, and Marty McGuinn of Mellon. None was autocratic, but they set the agenda firmly.

Twice a year, I presented my proposed legislative priorities to the Board. The first four times, they added financial literacy to the list.
I thought they were just trying to be nice. What could I do about financial literacy?

The fifth time, the mild-mannered CEOs got a little testy and said, "We told you financial literacy was a priority. When are you going to do something about it?"

Gulp. Okay, I get it.

Then I met the single most charismatic person I have ever met: John Hope Bryant, founder of Operation HOPE. He had met most of my CEOs but had not gained as much traction as he needed. Operation HOPE provided financial counseling one-on-one and in classrooms, in twenty-five to thirty locations, mostly on the West Coast. But John had big dreams. Big dreams.

Our first event together was in Oakland. He had negotiated a "bank within a bank" at a BankWest branch. The idea was that when a customer didn't know how to improve their credit score, balance a checking account, or start a business, the bank personnel sent them across the lobby to Operation HOPE.

The grand opening featured, drum roll please, Secretary of the Treasury John Snow. No kidding.

As I introduced John Bryant to my CEOs and invited him to our meetings, the CEOs began a little friendly competition to outdo one another.

Then came the big one. John called to say he was starting a HOPE Center at Ebenezer Baptist Church, the home church of Martin Luther King Sr. and Jr.

He needed five million dollars to complete it.

I made six phone calls and got five million dollars.

Today, Operation HOPE is in 4,000 school systems, has provided financial education to one million students, and operates in 285 bank branches. Its annual budget is fifty million dollars.

We didn't "solve the problem," but through Operation HOPE, the Roundtable had a significant impact on millions of lives. A good day's work.

Better financial literacy for all is purpose enough.

***AH HA!* John Hope Bryant, plus one hundred banks, can change lives.**

16,000 Phone Calls and 30 Iowans!

Remember the $5,000 IRA and $15,000 401(k)? Tougher uphill climb than I thought.

The problem was that this issue was a mile wide and an inch thick. Congressmen who sponsored the IRA and 401(k) bill always put out a press release and sometimes even held a Town Hall to tout it, but they never took any real action.

The real opposition came from what I called "Treasury Gnomes." Those second and third level officials always made sure IRA expansion never made it into the final bill. They liked taxes and disliked tax cuts.

Then George W. Bush announced his 2002 Tax Cut Bill. We were not in it, but we found sponsors to attach the IRA and 401(k) provision as it moved through Congress. It was quietly understood, however, that the provision would be dropped in Conference. No fuss, no muss.

I went to Edward Jones, a member company that would be positively affected and whose clients were clamoring for it. Ten thousand agents, in every single congressional district. Through their government affairs director, the soft-spoken but relentless Mike Esser, they offered to call their congressmen. Mike told the agents not to do anything except call congressmen and report to him daily in a virtual rally session.

These agents made phone calls for a living. They made sixteen thousand phone calls in ten days. Majority Leader Trent Lott called personally and demanded I stop the calls. House Ways and Means Chair Bill Thomas simply turned off his phones.

The first step was to get it into the "chairman's mark." That meant that to take it out, someone would have to make a motion to remove it.

Senator Charles Grassley was chairman of the conference committee, and I asked his chief of staff if he would meet with thirty Iowa constituents. Of course he agreed.

My lobbyist, Scott Talbott, a brilliant guy, identified thirty Iowans who cared about this: small bankers, credit unions, John Deere employees, teachers, and bank branch managers. We flew them to Washington, D.C.

Then we found a bill Senator Grassley had sponsored two years earlier that did exactly this. Lisa bought radio spots in four Iowa media markets with John Philip Sousa music, thanking "our hero Charles Grassley" for increasing IRAs and 401(k)s to help senior citizens.

When he came into the meeting, I played the radio spot. His staff literally grabbed my wrist to stop the tape. Grassley said, "I want to hear this."

When it ended, he smiled and said, "Well, I guess we have to pass this now."

Today, forty-six percent of Americans have 401(k)s or IRAs, with $27.7 trillion in assets. I think that CEO got more than his five cents per share.

My purpose was straightforward: to allow average Americans to save for their own retirement.

_AH HA!_ Sometimes democracy needs a little nudge.

Get Yourself to California

And then there was saving the Fair Credit Reporting Act, known as the FCRA. Essentially, if you borrowed money and didn't pay it back on time, you got a bad credit score, and the next time you borrowed money, it would cost more.

Eighty percent of Americans hated it. But the FCRA and a national credit score ensured that merchants could lend money and expect to be repaid. Borrowers could get loans based on their actual credit history.

What made it all work was that it was uniform in all fifty states. Lenders could be confident you hadn't defaulted on a car loan in another state.

The problem was that the uniform national standard was expiring. And if it expired, the national credit system would collapse.

We pulled out all the stops: a CEO task force, mobilizing the 4:00 p.m. Monday sessions with bank lobbyists, face-to-face meetings in Washington and in home districts with key members of Congress, even video interviews with car dealers.

We were making progress, and then disaster struck. California was preparing its own version of credit reporting, which was completely unworkable. If California adopted its version before Congress renewed the federal law, Congress would take the easy way out and adopt California's version.

Once again, the iconic Richard Kovacevich came to the rescue. I traveled to Sacramento and spent a week with the bank lobbyists in California. They handed me my hat and told me, "Don't let the door hit you in the ass." They didn't need Washington's help.

Worse, their "plan" was to put the issue to a referendum. In California. Guess how that would turn out.

On a conference call the following Monday morning, I reported to Kovacevich and the other CEOs that there was nothing I could do. The bank lobbyists had thrown me out.

Wrong. In a quiet voice, Mr. Kovacevich said, "Be in my office tomorrow at eight a.m. Then drive to Sacramento and tell them I sent you. If anyone doesn't like it, they can call me directly."

I did exactly that, and by the end of the following week, the California bank lobbyists got religion, and we got a reasonable bill. Oh, we had to hire a big-time constitutional lawyer and sue them to get the worst parts out, but that's another story.

My purpose was for America to have a uniform credit reporting system, ensuring that, to this day, you get the credit score you earn.

AH HA! **Get yourself to California and bring the big Kovacevich Stick.**

It All Comes Crashing Down: Creating HOPE NOW

It was the spring of 2007, and I was in the catbird's seat. The public actually appreciated banks and other financial services companies (hard to believe). The economy was good, homeownership was at an all-time high, I had one hundred loyal members, my CEOs loved me, and I was respected in D.C.

Life was good. But it wouldn't stay that way.

My first hint that something was amiss came in May 2007. Tom James, CEO of Raymond James, called me and said, "Bartlett, you are in big trouble." Huh?

He explained, "I decided to buy some of those mortgage-backed securities (MBS) to get a higher return. So I called my friend Richard Fuld, CEO of Lehman Brothers (Lehman was not a member, thank God), and bought an option on $1 billion of MBS for $100,000. I sent my guys to New York to audit these MBS.

"This morning, my team called from New York to report that these MBS were underwater, but Lehman didn't know it. Less than 70 percent of the mortgages were solvent.

"I told my team to come home, called Fuld, and told him to keep the $100,000. He told me I was the first buyer to audit the book. Then I called you.

"I don't know when, but this is going to collapse the economy. Thought you ought to know."

Puzzling over that, I decided to ask what a "2/28" mortgage was. It meant a homeowner would buy a home at a 2 percent interest rate for two years, and then the mortgage rate would jump to 11 percent. Consumer groups aptly named them "exploding mortgages." When I learned that, I was sick to my stomach.

By July 2008, the foreclosures started with ferocity. And worse, whoever originated the mortgages had long since sold them to Lehman and others, who divided them into tranches and sold the tranches.

In the third week of August, Secretary of the Treasury Hank Paulson called my colleague, the revered John Dalton, former Secretary of the Navy and the head of the Housing Policy Council, a division of the Roundtable. He said, "Foreclosures are out of control, and you've got to come up with a plan to do something about it. And George W. Bush will announce your plan from the White House next Friday at 2:00 p.m."

John and I got permission from my Board, hired a D.C. mortgage expert, the brilliant Faith Schwartz, set initial criteria for modifications, secured a toll-free number (888-HOPE-NOW), retained a phone bank to receive and route the incoming calls, created a governance structure, and obtained commitments from CEOs for $5 million.

When the president announced it, the correct 888 number appeared on the screen, but he read it out loud as 1-800-HOPE-NOW. Oops. But our phones rang off the wall.

Of course, we couldn't simply forgive the mortgages, but we set up a system that, if the homeowner had any appreciable income, we would waive all the past-due fees and provide a mortgage that fit the income. Sounds simple, but it wasn't. If there was no income, we offered a financially painless solution, rather than face a foreclosure.

In four years, we modified 7.5 million mortgages. As bad as the Great Recession was, I'm convinced that if we hadn't saved those 7.5 million from foreclosure, the country would have taken a long time to recover.

Of course, my banks never received credit for this, but HOPE Now averted a larger disaster and saved 7.5 million families from foreclosure.

We couldn't save them all, but 7.5 million families kept their homes and paid their mortgages, and that was my purpose.

***AH HA!* In a crisis, do what you have to do.**

The Great Recession

We created HOPE Now in August 2007. It helped 7.5 million homeowners, but the mortgage crisis had bled into the overall economy, and the Great Recession was on.

In October 2007, my Board adopted a resolution that essentially said: "No member of the Roundtable shall originate a mortgage unless the borrower has the capacity to pay the full term of the mortgage."

Sounds simple, but it went to the heart of the problem. It took me until January 2008 to get all members to sign this policy. The last one was Countrywide. I flew to California to get the signature, and it was testy. Too late, but at least I had the satisfaction that they would not be adding to the problem going forward.

Because these trillions of dollars of tranches of mortgage-backed securities were embedded throughout the financial infrastructure and were uncollectable at face value, the economy tanked.

Fannie Mae and Freddie Mac, AIG, Lehman, Countrywide, WAMU, Bear Stearns, Wachovia, and Merrill Lynch all either failed or were acquired for pennies on the dollar.

In September 2008, we held our annual conference in Washington. Midmorning, I noticed the cell phones buzzing. Apparently, the global money market system had collapsed. It was called "broke the buck." Several CEOs, with fear in their eyes, told me they had to leave. Right then.

Treasury Secretary Hank Paulson was a champion. To stop the run on the money market system, he called an emergency press conference to announce that the U.S. Treasury would stand behind the money markets. Did he have the authority to do that? We'll never know, but he stopped the run.

He went to Congress and forced through the infamous TARP, literally getting on one knee and begging Nancy Pelosi to pass it.

He summoned fifteen of my CEOs to the Treasury and ordered them to accept their share of TARP money to stabilize the economy. When they protested that they didn't need the money, he told them they had to accept it, or else.

Two weeks later, Jamie Dimon, CEO of JPMorgan Chase, presented a check for $25 million plus interest to pay it back. Paulson was not amused. He told him to put the check back in his pocket.

All of 2007, 2008, and 2009 was a nightmare for the banking industry, both financially and reputation-wise. The worst three years of my professional life.

The good news is my CEOs stuck with me, and I stuck with them. I retired at the end of 2012 after we got Dodd-Frank, the cleanup legislation, for better or worse.

I was exhausted but satisfied that I had done my duty.

My purpose was for the banks to survive, and rebuild.

_AH HA!_ When the world is collapsing around you, get out of the way.

Paying for HOPE Now

I've told you that HOPE Now succeeded in preventing foreclosures for 7.5 million homeowners and providing them with mortgages they could afford. And we stood it up from concept to implementation in less than a week.

With the superb leadership of Secretary Dalton and Faith Schwartz, HOPE Now received calls from desperate homeowners in foreclosure, gathered the necessary information, and introduced the homeowner to the right bank via a "warm transfer." ("Mrs. Johnson, on the line is Bill with your bank, who can help you. I have electronically sent him your information. I will stay on the line as you two get to know each other.")

Faith also had to secure a common modification agreement that all the banks would accept. It was called a "Waterfall," with ten steps to reach a conclusion. Complicated? Yes. And she handled it quickly and with grace.

We had been in operation for three weeks when Secretary Dalton showed up unannounced in my office and said, "Boss, we've got a problem."

None of the banks had signed the contract agreeing to the standard modifications, the "Waterfall." Worse, none had sent the funds to pay for it. Not one. We had already approved 5,000 mortgage modifications and spent a million dollars.

It seemed the contracts and funding were stuck in the respective General Counsels' offices, and their unanimous answer was a firm "No."

When in doubt, call the CEOs. At that moment, I called James Wells, CEO of SunTrust in Atlanta. "Jim, do you trust me?"

"Well, sure," he replied.

"I want you to do something totally unheard of: sign the contract I will fax to you without asking your General Counsel. And wire me $1 million within an hour."

Jim replied, "You're going to get me fired, but I'll do it."

Within five days, all the CEOs had followed Jim's lead and done the same: Wells, Wachovia, U.S. Bank, Bank of America, BB&T, Citi, every single one.

Four weeks later, I learned that the General Counsel for the group representing the mortgage-backed securities (remember the tranches?) was being uncooperative. Faith invited him to a meeting in my offices to work out the differences.

She also invited the eight operating heads of our call centers from Kansas City, Houston, and elsewhere to come to my office to negotiate the details.

This guy, whose name I choose to forget, barreled in and loudly announced that he was not going to agree to anything.

At the end of my rope, I said, "Everyone wait here for fifteen minutes. I'm going to go get this guy fired."

I called Tim Ryan, head of SIFMA and my counterpart for securities. Tim called this guy's boss, and he was much more agreeable.

Our purpose was to help ourselves and our country out of the Great Recession.

_AH HA!_ In a crisis, you have to act boldly and quickly!

Face the Cameras, and Smile!

As the Great Recession wound down, I had one more mountain to climb. And it wasn't big legislation like Gramm-Leach-Bliley or Class Action Reform. Those days were over.

Nor was it defeating Dodd-Frank, or even trimming it back. I told my CEOs early on that it was not possible.

The challenge was to restore the banks' reputation.

We had to tell our story to the American people through the media. Bank CEOs, cautioned by their lawyers, had been reluctant to do that.

I told the CEOs to publicly embrace the new regulations. Several times, I used the phrase "Hug your regulator." Got a few funny looks from that one.

But the big turn, beginning in 2009, was to communicate directly with the public. Bankers historically avoided the spotlight.

Very few of them gave interviews or went on television. All through 2008, I told them often that they had to change if they were to survive. They had to put themselves into the public eye and tell their story. Talk about the small business loans they made, the communities they served, the homeowners they saved, and the good they did. Most were uncomfortable doing that. It's not "bank-like."

Then we caught a break. In the fall of 2009, the fifteen biggest bank CEOs were summoned to the White House so President Obama could literally take them to the woodshed about credit card practices. The public hated credit cards at the time, but everyone had a wallet full.

The meeting was at 10:00 a.m. At 8:00 a.m., I invited my CEOs to the old Riggs Bank Conference Room on Pennsylvania Avenue, half a block from the West Wing entrance, for breakfast. I told them it was a setup so the president could look tough by "beating up" on the bankers.

I advised them to stroll down Pennsylvania Avenue in small groups of two or three to avoid the appearance of big, powerful bankers.

Then I told them there was no way out of the West Wing except through a wall of TV cameras and reporters. They were shocked and somewhat fearful. Several told me I was wrong, that the White House had promised "off the record."

I then gave them a one-hour tutorial on how to turn and confidently face the cameras. Take every question and answer forthrightly. Tell your story about the good things you do for your customers and communities. Smile.

And don't leave the White House grounds until the last reporter has asked the last question.

They responded like champions. Richard Davis of U.S. Bank, John Stumpf of Wells Fargo, Bob Kelly of Bank of New York Mellon, Jamie Dimon of JPMorgan Chase, Jim Wells of SunTrust, Kelly King of BB&T, and Ken Thompson of Wachovia. They knew their stuff and confidently described what they did for their customers and communities.

They stayed on the West Wing grounds until 2:30 p.m., seeking out interviews. It was the first good press big banks had received in five years.

After that, most of my CEOs accepted and sought out every press interview, print and broadcast, they could find: CNN, CNBC, CBS, *The New York Times*, *The Washington Post*, local channels, and newspapers.

Within a year or two, we started to regain a somewhat positive reputation with the American people.

And, oh yes, as an industry, with the help of Congress, we corrected most of the credit card abuses for which President Obama had called them out.

My purpose was to tell the banks' story. And I needed the CEOs for that.

***AH HA!* You've got to tell your own story.**

AN EPILOGUE

A Never Trumper Asks: "How Did We Get Here?"

When I started ***AH HA!*** in late Spring of 2024, I had no plan to write a chapter about Donald Trump. I was one of the original "Never Trumpers," signing Mickey Edwards' (former GOP congressman from Oklahoma) original letter with about twenty other former Republican Congressmen in September 2016. I voted Libertarian that year, and endorsed Biden in 2020. Not proud of that vote in hindsight. Hell, I thought he was a Centrist and reasonably competent.

In 2024, I added my voice urging Biden to step aside. And I somewhat reluctantly voted for Kamala Harris, only because she was not Trump.

And throughout, I maintained postings on LinkedIn and, to anyone who asked, described Donald Trump as a disaster.

But even as I watched the ongoing disaster in slow motion, I couldn't believe that an indicted and convicted felon, and the instigator of an insurrection to overthrow the government, would actually be elected.

Boy, was I wrong.

So, as I write this in the Summer of 2025, six months into the Trump disaster, I will try to share a perspective of a proud Republican and believer in the free market, the Rule of Law, and the Constitution. I will try to make some predictions, but I fear that the state of the union for the next three and a half years is likely to be a far worse disaster than anyone can predict today.

Being a natural optimist, I'm reluctant to predict how bad it's going to be.

***AH HA!* Hang on pardner, it's going to be a wild ride.**

Would Anyone Here Make a Loan to This Guy?

I was vaguely aware of Donald Trump before his emergence as a force. He was an unpleasant reality TV host, the subject of frequent bankruptcies that never seemed to affect him, a curmudgeon with multiple wives, a bigger-than-life guy you'd never want to meet.

One of my internal rules about campaign contributions when I was in charge of the Roundtable PAC was that we would never contribute unless the candidate met the "Bring Home to Mama" test. Meaning, someone on the committee would have to say he would be willing to bring the candidate home to meet his family.

Donald Trump would never have met that test on his best day.

But one of my jobs at the Roundtable was to anticipate, indeed, predict the future.

In early 2015, I started to notice this strange guy in the Republican presidential primary. Not really part of the main group, but off to the side, throwing rocks at the others. Generally disruptive. Breaking all the rules.

So I was briefing my CEOs on the GOP primary: Jeb Bush, John Kasich, Newt Gingrich, Chris Christie, Carly Fiorina, Marco Rubio, Bobby Jindal, Rand Paul, even Ted Cruz. All serious politicos. All with a claim to the nomination.

And then there was Trump. "Who is this guy?"

Well, "this guy" had a shtick that set them up and knocked them down. He broke all the rules without breaking a sweat.

So, in briefing my CEOs on the GOP primary, I described the odds and outlook for each of the serious candidates. Getting to Trump last, I asked a question:

"I don't know what to tell you about Donald Trump. He shouldn't even be in this race, but he seems to be picking up steam. So, I'll ask you. You are all bankers and are always looking for a good deal.

Would any of you loan money to this guy under any circumstances?"

Not a hand went up. And no one even changed expression. These were the biggest bankers in America.

"Why not?"

Answer: "'Cause he wouldn't pay us back."

And that was my introduction to Donald J. Trump.

***AH HA!* If you wouldn't bring them home to Mama, or loan them money for a new car, don't vote for them.**

Reagan vs. Trump

I admit my political hero is Ronald Reagan. Principled, forthright, always seeking to do the right thing. I didn't necessarily start there. I grew up in Texas, a Bush Republican, and still admire him. But Ronald Reagan won me over with his actions and principles.

Kind to others at all times. Never raised his voice, but never backed down from doing the right thing either.

He understood capitalism, the Constitution, the Republican Party, the give and take of making laws, and the need to stand on principle.

And he was unwaveringly kind and courteous.

He saw the big picture and focused on making it come true.

A man of integrity.

In short, Reagan was everything Trump is not.

And it's not just compared to Reagan. Trump doesn't measure up to any of my political heroes: John Tower, Phil Gramm, George H. W. Bush, George W. Bush, Bob Dole, Tom Loeffler, Trent Lott, Bill Frenzel, Howard Baker, Bill Clements, Bob Bullock, Lynn Martin, Leon Panetta, Jack Kemp, Mickey Edwards, Bob Folsom. The list goes on.

All had their flaws, of course, but how can I say this? Donald Trump is *all* flaws.

Given where I've been and who I have known and been close to, of course, I would be a "Never Trumper." I couldn't have been anything else.

Ronald Reagan and the others I named were no shrinking violets.

Their purpose was to do what was best for America.

AH HA! **It's all about character.**

The Flyover Country Revolts

In late 2015, I started asking my friends from "outside the Beltway" what they thought of Trump, expecting them to reply, "I can't stand him," or something similar. That's not what I heard. Even my revered Lunch Bunch was evenly divided. I regret to say this, but I had been in Washington too long.

Republican friends in Texas, and even some Democrats, described their support for Trump in pretty much the same way: "I'm tired of the elites on the East and West coasts looking down their noses at me." A prominent, very smart Dallas lawyer said he hated, just hated, being talked down to by New York lawyers who were not as smart as he was, but who were always condescending. "If they weren't paying me such good money, I would punch them in the nose."

Another recalled a late-night episode, Jon Stewart or some other host, laughing on the air about flying across the country and taking a leak over the Flyover States. They all laughed.

In fact, in 2016 I saw one report that summed up our cultural divide: every county in America with a Whole Foods voted for Hillary Clinton; every county in America with a Cracker Barrel Old Country Store voted for Trump. Pretty well sums it up.

The whole Flyover thing came out of the shadows in the last week of the campaign when Hillary Clinton made fun of Trump voters by calling them "the deplorables." That single snark sealed her defeat.

AH HA! **Make fun of me, will you?**

The Bible as a Prop, or a Weapon

All in all, Donald Trump's first term was annoying, sometimes frightening, disruptive, harmful to individuals like the Joint Chiefs of Staff, added exponentially to the national debt, and harmful to respect for America overseas.

But all in all, no permanent harm was done. Well, not much anyway. More akin to Andrew Jackson than to any other former president.

Perhaps the worst moment, at least for me, was his expropriation of the Bible (borrowed from a White House staffer) to shake it in the air and shout his anger at peaceful demonstrators during the George Floyd protests in front of the White House. That was the worst for me because he used Christianity to foment hate. Quite an un-Christian thing to do in my book.

But America would survive.

Then came December 10, after he lost the election, when he called out his legions to come to Washington on January 6 to overthrow the elected government. He literally tweeted the words, "Come to Washington on January 6. It's going to be wild."

He sent that tweet to the Proud Boys and others from the White House immediately after a four-hour Oval Office briefing with Rudy Giuliani and others who laid out a plan to overturn the election by pressuring Vice President Pence (in the shadow of a gallows) to refuse to certify the Electoral College ballots.

And they came, assaulted Capitol Police, stormed the Capitol, and for hours prevented the counting of the ballots and the peaceful transition of power.

January 6, 2021, became the first attempted insurrection of the U.S. government since the Civil War.

Sadly, overthrowing the elected government was their purpose.

AH HA! **It's going to be wild.**

Four Years Later, The New Trump Arrives with a Vengeance!

I won't recite all the reasons Trump won the election, because he won it fair and square. He did everything right, mainly by enraging his 48 percent base.

And amazingly, the Democrats did everything wrong. Starting with opening the southern border to 2.6 million illegal immigrants a year, and pretending they had no choice.

But the elephant in the room, pardon the expression, was their refusal to acknowledge what was obvious to anyone who watched television: that Joe Biden was frail and could not handle the job now, much less for four more years.

The Democratic leaders (Schumer, Jeffries, Coons, Durbin, Pelosi, Barack Obama, and others) could have quietly but firmly asked him to step aside in January 2024. Only Democratic Congressman Dean Phillips had the backbone to tell the truth and run against Biden in the primaries.

Except for Phillips, it was far from "Profiles in Courage."

And here is the contrast. On August 7, 1974, House Republican Leader John Rhodes, Senate Republican Leader Hugh Scott, and 1964 GOP presidential nominee Barry Goldwater went to the White House. Face to face in the Oval Office, they told Richard Nixon he must resign or be impeached. He resigned the next day.

One uncomfortable meeting in January 2024, and the Democrats could have nominated a credible candidate and saved the country from the agony that was coming.

Then came the "face-plant" debate. Biden didn't actually fall, but he may as well have.

Still, the Democrats refused to tell the president it was over. Only Nancy Pelosi stood strong and told President Biden he needed to step aside. Kamala Harris tried to put together a campaign, but it was too late.

The result of that failure of courage by the Democratic leadership was a President Trump who is leading the country to perdition. I write this after 180 days. The stock market is good, but we are headed for a recession, tariffs that will lead to inflation and empty store shelves on an unprecedented scale, 260,000 federal employees fired, Zelensky humiliated and Putin honored, Canada and Greenland threatened, our allies driven away, and very significant public violations of the law.

And that's just the first six months. What bizarre kind of purpose is that?

AH HA! **This is not going to end well.**

Tariffs Explained

Lots of chaos in the first six months. Not all events so far are negative, but we are on a collision course: negative GDP in Q1, the rule of law under threat, deportations of U.S. citizens without hearings, a recession on the horizon, massive tariffs on our allies, inflation returning, and much more.

But for purposes of the book, since I am writing this as a snapshot in time, I will take a philosophical look at tariffs as a concept.

The American culture has always included a segment of the population that is anti-trade, choosing not to understand the immense value of international trade, especially the value to Americans.

Remember "the great sucking sound" of Ross Perot, the Smoot-Hawley Tariff that directly causing the Great Depression, or even the War of 1812, which was fought over trade policy.

Let's go back to basics. Even the term "trade deficit" is dangerously misleading. We use the same word "deficit" to describe something entirely different and far more serious: the fiscal deficit. With a fiscal deficit, the United States spends more than it takes in, borrows the difference, and creates inflation that can lead to bankruptcy.

But that is not the trade deficit. It just happens to use the same word.

Consider this: when I buy a shirt at Kohl's, I am operating a "deficit" with Kohl's. I buy a shirt but have nothing to sell to them. When Kohl's buys one thousand shirts from a company in Vietnam, it creates a "deficit" since Kohl's has nothing to sell to Vietnam.

But no harm is done. I am better off, Kohl's is better off, and Vietnam is better off.

It is the same with iPhones, soybeans, tractors, avocados, and beaver hats in the 1700s. In trade, whether cross-town or cross-border, all parties win, or they would not trade.

Of course, sometimes countries engage in predatory "dumping," meaning they subsidize a company or industry to buy market share. That is illegal under the WTO, but it takes years to enforce. Meanwhile, the American purchaser benefits from lower prices.

China engages in dumping and provides special subsidies. So does America. Think soybeans or the twenty-billion-dollar Intel subsidy.

Is trade good for China? Yes. And it is equally good for America, France, Korea, and South Africa.

American companies alone sell two hundred billion dollars in products and services to China every year. Stop that trade, and employees and shareholders of those companies would suffer quickly and dramatically.

International trade is the sum of millions of individuals making decisions to buy or sell. Each transaction is a good one, or they would not make it.

Trade is good for America, for China, for Chile, and for France.

The purpose of trade is to benefit both buyer and seller, or they would not trade.

AH HA! **Trade is good, and more trade is better.**

So, What to Do?

Things may change, but the current culture wars have been twenty years in the making, and change is not likely unless we make systemic changes in the electoral process.

It does not have to be this way. I served in Congress for eight years, with really contentious issues and strong views on all sides: Social Security reform, NAFTA, the ADA, Reagan budget cuts, the 1986 tax bill, immigration reform, and the Strategic Defense Initiative. The debate could get heated, but it was never dysfunctional. And the rule of law always prevailed.

2025 is new territory. Here are some ideas for a way forward. All are very challenging, but any of these could offer a path out of the chaos.

A new party capturing the center. *No Labels* tried and may one day succeed. Elon Musk's America Party shows some promise, for a few days.

A Congressional Caucus independent of the two parties. Twenty House members in an evenly divided House could force legislative compromise since they would hold the swing votes.

A "Top Two" Congressional election system. All candidates would run in the same election , and the top two would go to a runoff. Extremists would struggle to find votes in a runoff.

A "Ranked Choice" voting system. Voters choose their favorite, then rank the remaining candidates by preference. It has been used successfully in Alaska and Maine and tends to move candidates toward the center to capture second and third-place votes. It is not perfect. Ranked-choice voting once nominated a democratic socialist as mayor of New York City, but it also helped elect Senators Susan Collins and Lisa Murkowski.

Term limits. Ten years for House members and twelve years for senators. This would likely require a state-led constitutional convention, since Congress will never vote to limit itself.

A Reagan or Roosevelt-style presidential candidate to lead us out of the wilderness. Frankly, I would settle for Eisenhower.

Ban corporate contributions and dark money. Candidates should raise campaign funds the old-fashioned way—from individuals—and report every contribution.

Burn the House. A Democratic takeover of the House and Senate could allow the GOP to start over. It would carry risks and unintended consequences, but it might be necessary.

Reform and rebuild the once-honorable Republican Party. John Danforth, Michael Steele, Adam Kinzinger, Greg Wilson, and a handful of others are trying through the Republican Legacy project. Their efforts currently lack energy, but at least they are trying.

Any or all of these institutional reforms could help slow the spiral into chaos. But all require courage, persistence, diligence, leadership, and vision. And we seem to be lacking in all of those areas.

Our collective purpose should be to restore a democratic system that works, with decency.

AH HA! **The solutions are available, but only if we grab them.**

MENTORING! THE JOY OF MY LIFE

Discovering Mentoring

I suppose I have always mentored, in a casual way. Meaning I take an interest in friends, colleagues, and employees for coaching. I recall a number of colleagues from City Hall, Congress, and the Roundtable who still stay in touch and ask for advice.

But I didn't start serious mentoring until about 2012. And since then, I have mentored over a dozen people seriously.

Once I started, the word spread. Someone would confide in a friend that they were struggling with life choices and didn't know where to look for help. And the friend would say something like, "Well, I know a guy who knows a guy who does a little counseling over his kitchen table. He doesn't charge anything, but I can check and see if he can help."

The initial question is usually pretty narrow: how do I find the right job, college, or internship? But the conversation usually moves from there to more "life" questions. About half of my mentees, whom I describe here by first name, I still mentor for big life decisions, but most are one-shot: getting into the right college or landing the right job.

The first session usually takes about two hours: what are you trying to achieve, what do you have to offer, and what are your barriers?

Then, toward the end of the two hours, I give them their homework assignment: sometime in the next two weeks, set aside a four-hour reflection time. Go to your favorite place to be alone, a park, a favorite coffee shop, somewhere quiet. By yourself, with only a legal pad or a laptop, write down what you want your life to look like in ten years: financial, family, income, education, geography, and home.

State your purpose. Write it down.

Be specific. Meaning, how much money do you want to have in the bank? What income? Where do you want to live? Small town or big city? Describe your ideal married or relationship life.

Then wait a week and schedule a two-hour session in the same place, and answer the same question for two years from now.

Then we get down to business and set regular meeting times to make a plan and review progress.

The regular meetings fit their schedule and comfort level. Sometimes weekly, usually more like every two to four weeks. But at the end of every session, we always decide on the next time and place.

And every step has to be consistent with the ten- and two-year vision.

It is remarkable how answering that question: *What is my purpose?* or *What do I want my life to be in ten years?* will focus one's goals.

AH HA! **First, decide where you are going, then you'll know what road to take.**

Lalo, My First

I started with Lalo in 2012, the year I was retiring from the Roundtable. I think he was fourteen. He had a terrible home life and school life. I inherited Lalo from my daughter Allison and her husband Brett, who sponsored him in Big Brothers and Big Sisters.

Lalo was in the "Alternative School," meaning he had been kicked out of regular schools for grades, behavior, or maybe worse. I recall that during our first year, he told me he had gone to his best friend's funeral, a gang shooting.

We met every two weeks for breakfast at 7:30 a.m. He never missed and was never late. I asked him once why he stuck with me even though I "busted his chops," as he put it. He said, "Because you are the only adult who has ever talked with me about anything."

Once he started studying and got away from the gangs, he graduated valedictorian from the Alternative School, joined the Air Force, got married, got divorced, crashed his credit score, tried being an electrician, and did a dozen other things.

Lalo has now stabilized his life. We talk a couple of times a month. Last year, he identified and stated his purpose: to move into a career with consistent earnings and solid job prospects. He enrolled in a commercial driving school, graduated at the top of his class, and started a job as a commercial driver.

It's a new start, and he is following his purpose.

He also has a stable relationship with a good woman, a savings account, and an improving credit score.

I've stuck with him for twelve years, and he has stuck with me, through good and bad. And I'm glad I did.

His purpose is to build a good life.

***AH HA!* Sometimes it takes a little longer.**

Belen, Lalo's Sister

Belen is Lalo's older sister, whom I also inherited from Allison and Brett. She didn't have as many challenges as Lalo, but she had her own struggles with a disruptive home life.

She and I met regularly over the course of five or six years, usually for breakfast. I helped her get into George Mason University and find a part-time job. She made it through two years, maybe a little more, before she drifted away. That's okay, two years of college is better than none.

A big step for her was gaining the self-confidence to look for a job. We spent about three hours at a Denny's, practicing how to walk into a room with confidence, make eye contact, shake hands firmly, and say her name clearly. Ah, the things they don't teach you in school.

We also did a little "relationship" counseling along the way. She's now married with a child. I don't hear from her much, but I'm glad I was able to help her during a crucial time in her life. **And that was my purpose**

***AH HA!* Sometimes just a little bit of help goes a long way.**

Alice, from Rwanda to West Texas to the IMF

And then there was Alice. On my first mission trip to African New Life Mission (ANLM) in Rwanda, I let it be known that I would like to sponsor a student. "Sponsor" is the process that ANLM uses to fund the schools, meaning the sponsor pays $36 per month in tuition.

When I met Pastor Charles, the founder of ANLM, I mentioned that I was hoping for a smart student who could really succeed. "Oh, you want Alice. She may be president of Rwanda one day."

And thus, for $36 a month, I became a lifetime sponsor of Alice. She graduated at the top of her class and told me she wanted to go to college in America, which is pretty rare. Through Zoom, I coached her for over a year. She faced multiple rejections and lots of barriers, but she never gave up.

She enrolled at Hardin-Simmons University in Abilene, Texas, and Gail and I drove her from DFW to Abilene. Alice had never been more than thirty miles from Kigali and found herself at an almost all-white school in West Texas.

From Africa to Abilene. A culture shock, to say the least. She studied, made A's, and even worked on campus in construction during the hot Texas summer.

Her passion was international development, so I arranged for her to stay in a basement apartment in Northern Virginia while she looked for a job in Washington, D.C. I coached her on networking, but she did the work herself. She landed a position at the coveted International Monetary Fund and earned two promotions in her first two years. She is now studying for her master's degree at night.

She and I talk regularly, and she often visits my family on holidays.

Alice knows her purpose: to improve lives globally. I believe Alice could be president of Rwanda one day, or head of the United Nations. And I can say I knew her when.

***AH HA!* Never give up on your dreams.**

Chely, the Most Focused Person I Know

She was seventeen years old when Gail, Allison, and I met her. She was seated at our table for the graduation dinner for Phillips Academy, a charter school designed for foster children. She was so natural, mature, and pleasant. I only found out later her story: she jumped out the back window of her home on the edge of the jungle in Guatemala as soldiers machine-gunned her family, walked to the Rio Grande, and hitchhiked to Northern Virginia speaking no English. She was placed with a foster family and graduated at the top of her class.

She ran cross-country even though she had to borrow the shoes.

Such was her determination to succeed that she never even noticed the barriers. She just kept her eye on the next goal.

I met with her monthly for breakfast coaching for years. She wrote down everything I said and reported back the next month on what she had done. She put herself through George Mason while working more than twenty hours a week (okay, I helped a little), found Mr. Wonderful and married him, learned from Gail and me during our marriage coaching sessions, graduated *summa cum laude*, joined the board of directors for Phillips, and now has a fast-track career as a frontline supervisor in a technology company. She will be a CEO one day.

Chely has always, always known her purpose. And she acts on it.

AH HA! Grit with a smile

Megan, a Smile... and a Brain

Megan is one of those rare people with a brilliant IQ combined with natural empathy, or EQ. And she is deeply focused on achieving her purpose.

But in 2006, she had no idea what that purpose was. Her mother called to say, "Megan is lost. Can she come live with you? You and Gail can give her some direction."

She did, and we did. Every night over the dinner table, she explored one idea after another. (And Gail helped dress her appropriately every morning.)

After two years, it all came together. She landed a top job in her field, moved out, and began an incredibly productive career. As she faced career choices, she always called me to discuss the pros and cons and how to land the position.

Her jobs all had Washington connections, so she often stayed with us.

Then came her thirtieth birthday. "Megan, remember your ten-year purpose: husband and family by your thirtieth birthday. You're not making progress." So we made a plan that involved a search on Match.com. Her first draft of her profile was awful, so I rewrote it for her. She was engaged to a doctor within ninety days. Megan and I call him "Dr. Wonderful."

At their wedding, I confessed, "It's true I wrote Megan's profile. And 80 percent of it is 100 percent true, or 100 percent is 80 percent true. You'll have to figure out which."

They are happily, truly happily, married with two adorable, well-adjusted children.

And she is now a senior executive on a fast-track career path. I'm embarrassed to tell you how much money she makes.

Megan still calls me for follow-on coaching.

For almost twenty years, my purpose was to offer a little coaching to a brilliant young woman and watch her soar.

AH HA! Megan the Wonder Woman.

Carson, My Ambitious Nephew

The only family member who sought or accepted my mentorship is Carson, the now twenty-year-old son of my nephew James. I didn't mind, as I accepted the adage of "prophet in his own land."

A dozen years ago, at a family reunion, I had counseled James and another nephew, John, on the value and techniques of investing in the stock market, which they took to with gusto.

Carson followed his father James's investing through the years. In his senior year of high school, he called me out of the blue and said, "Uncle Steve, I want to be rich and successful and stable like you. Will you teach me?"

So, with his father's blessing, I started mentoring Carson. Not only in the stock market, but also in life choices, values, hard work, a good career, integrity, education, and doing right. We started with his ten-year vision, of course. We talk regularly.

Carson is marrying his high school sweetheart, owns a good house and a truck, and works full-time (with plenty of overtime) as a lineman for a power company. He has strong values and does right.

Carson is following his purpose and often freshens it.

AH HA! Satisfaction.

Emily, Overachieving Niece

Emily never actually asked me to mentor her, so this is a stretch. But I kind of fell into giving her career advice after her high school graduation. She sometimes asks, she always listens, and she is equally comfortable accepting, modifying, or rejecting my advice.

It started when she asked where to go to culinary school. I recommended a really expensive (go for the best) culinary institute. She laughed, saying, "We're country folks," and enrolled in community college, where she got an excellent culinary education almost free.

Staying in the food business, she went to work for Whole Foods. One Christmas, she told me she was being promoted to assistant manager of the prepared foods department. I advised her to fire someone on her first day (the manager was a wuss) and coached her on how to do it. She did, and her reputation was set.

She now manages one of the most profitable Whole Foods stores in the nation and is headed for the executive ranks. I still coach her, and she still chooses to agree or not. We share Mavericks tickets and jointly decide how to coach the team.

We share a greater purpose than a winning basketball team.

AH HA! A true high achiever.

Lucas, My Cowboy Grandson

My big coaching moment with Lucas came when, at age fifteen, he called to ask if I could get him a job as a cowboy. "Nope," I said, "but I can teach you how."

He followed my script and landed a summer cowboy job on his seventy-fifth application. He worked as a cowboy for three summers. Then I gently suggested he could be a broke cowboy all his life, or he could go to college, go into business, get rich, buy his own ranch, and hire the cowboys.

He is now at Colorado State studying business.

His purpose is to get rich and buy his own ranch.

AH HA! The most likable cowboy you'll ever meet.

All the Other Grandchildren

I am close to each of my grandchildren and give them frequent advice. They always listen carefully and respectfully. And they take my advice when they agree. I am blessed.

Jocelyn, Amelie, Jocelyn, Scout, Lucas, Jackson, Ellie, Owen, and Lily, thank you for listening.

My purpose in life is to help and guide these grandchildren to live full and productive lives.

AH HA! Grandchildren: my true purpose in life.

David, Carolyn, Aubrey, Rebecca, Heather, Eli, Kelly, Michael, and So Many More

Word gets around, and they come to me. Usually these are short-term engagements: "How do I get a job?" "Where should I go to college?" "Why do I feel lost?"

It usually takes two to five sessions to resolve the current problem, and then they go on their way. Often, though, they report back to me later with their life successes.

I always make them start with one question: "What do you want your life to look like in ten years?" It has a way of focusing the mind.

_AH HA!_ Leave the light on, and people will find you.

God's Plan

I use the word "plan" instead of "purpose," because I believe God actually has a plan for us. We define our purpose and hope it fits into His plan.

Several times in this tome, I have referred to God's plan: a wake-up call, a choice, or unexpected circumstances that radically changed my life.

Do I think God has had a plan for my life? Well, yes. Just as I believe He has a plan for your life.

But more precisely, I believe God has good options for us at every stage of our lives. And He knows of options that are bad for us. We get to choose, and life's goal is to figure out God's plan as we make those choices. And then choose wisely.

Let me cite some specific instances in my life that I believe reflect God's plan:

In **November 1944**, my dad was pinned down in the Battle of the Hürtgen Forest, one of the most brutal infantry battles of the war and the longest in U.S. history. He stepped on a land mine that blew off his foot. He "persuaded" five German soldiers to carry him to a U.S. Army first aid station. No doubt in my mind, had he not stepped on that land mine, he would have been dead within two days. God's plan was for my Dad, and ultimately for me, to live.

In **1951**, Brooks Apparel of Los Angeles decided to open a plant in Texas. My father, one year out of USC and the youngest manager at the company, volunteered to open the plant. He had a wife and two young kids and had never been outside Los Angeles except to go to war. Had he not volunteered to move to Texas, I would have grown up in Los Angeles. I'm pretty sure that was not God's plan.

In **1962**, Dad lost his dream job at Brooks and got a new job in Dallas. Traumatic for the family, but if he had not left Brooks, I would have graduated from a small rural high school in Lockhart, Texas, and entered the 50,000-student University of Texas as a freshman, knowing no one. Least of all a ready-made political base, which I had when I entered UT from Dallas. God's plan was for my political head start at UT.

In **1964**, I needed $100 for Goldwater signs, and my best friend, Wick Allison, snapped his fingers at Gail Coke, eliciting her famous "Jump up my ass" retort. I instantly fell in love with her and invited her to share, and indeed guide, my life. Was "Jump up my ass" part of God's plan? I think so.

In **1965**, I stumbled under a lawnmower and my large toe was amputated. Had I not, I would have enlisted in the U.S. Army on my eighteenth birthday and found myself a second lieutenant in Vietnam during the Tet Offensive. No doubt in my mind, I would have been killed. That would not have been God's plan.

In **1972**, the regular pastor was on leave and asked Pastor Emeritus Walter Bennett to fill in. I heard Jesus' words, "If you love Me, feed My sheep," so clearly and so early in my life. Of course, that was God's plan.

In **1982**, I was mis-scheduled in the middle of a rainstorm and stumbled into a church chapel to pray. I heard God's warning to get ready for something really bad to happen. I faced the sudden loss of my Congressional District with calmness and won my election. God's voice. God's plan.

In **1983**, Rules Committee Chair Phil Burton had forgotten his promise to Esteban Torres, opening up a seat on Banking. Tom Loeffler also remembered that I wanted Education and Labor and the Disability Subcommittee. I became the Republican leader on disability issues, and those committee assignments gave me my eight years of serious legislating on disability, education, labor, banking, and housing. Dumb luck or God's plan? I think God's plan.

In **1991**, Bill Rathburn was the new police chief when I took office. He was ready to do things differently in Dallas. Without Bill Rathburn, new on the job and eager to change, Dallas could never have achieved that 40 percent reduction in violent crime. He was the essential ingredient. Thank you, Bill Rathburn, for being the instrument of God's plan.

In **1998**, Gail was gentle but firm with her career guidance. "You're a clever boy, you can figure it out." I changed course and found a golden opportunity in Washington. And kept my wife and marriage. Gail has always been the instrument of God's plan in my life.

In **1999**, the Roundtable was not a viable organization, only eighteen months from closing its doors. I took a chance and took the job. It was the career opportunity of a lifetime that God put in front of me—with Gail's help, of course.

In **early 2004**, at Immanuel Bible Church, I coincidentally sat behind Associate Pastor Michael Conner, who casually asked me what I was doing during a certain week that summer. I opened my calendar to prove I was way too busy. Surprise: that was the only week of the entire year I had no appointments. And my relationship with African New Life in Rwanda and my mentorship with Alice began. I don't know how He arranged it, but God cleared my calendar.

In the **summer of 2006**, I booked a whitewater raft trip down the Futaleufú River in southern Chile, all Class Four and Five rapids. On the first day, we were given a test in a Class Three rapid and told to "stay in the raft." Within thirty minutes, I was sucked to the bottom of the river, twenty feet down, but with a full life jacket. I looked up, saw the sky, planted my feet, and pushed up with all my strength. Nothing. Water was pouring on top of me, holding me down. Uh oh, this is trouble. I looked up, saw the sky, and what appeared to be God's face. "Swim downstream," He said clearly. I crawled along the bottom until the water released me.

On the last day, the guide explained that we faced three Class Fives, back to back to back. Looking at me, he said, "If you spill in the third one, you will probably live. If you spill in the second one, you might live. If you spill in the first one, you will die. You can walk around or take the raft." I walked around. God's plan, and God's voice.

In **2008**, I attended the annual banquet for Phillips School, and seventeen-year-old Chely Cifuentes was coincidentally at my table. My mentorship with her and her remarkable life have blossomed ever since. God's plan for both of us—for her to be at my table.

In **2009**, Walnut Springs Preserve placed an ad in *Texas Monthly* as the recession stopped the market, and our joyous retirement home in the

Texas Hill Country became a reality. That was the last ad they ever placed. Seems like God told them to place one more ad.

All God's plan. I truly believe that. God let me make the choices. Admittedly, I made some bad choices that were not in God's plan. But when I discovered and followed His plan, things turned out well.

Very well indeed.

I try to make my purpose God's purpose.

***AH HA!* God has a Plan. Our mission is to discover it.**

Three Excellent Children and Eight Beautiful Grandchildren

As I finish this book, filled with ***AH HA!*** moments, I realize the biggest ***AH HA!***'s of my life have been my three excellent children: Allison, Courtney, and Brian.

And my eight beautiful, adorable grandchildren: Jocelyn, Amelie, Scout, Lucas, Jackson, Ellie, Lily, and Owen.

They are each special in my life, and it is to their futures I dedicate this book.

Children and grandchildren are my legacy.

Daughters: Courtney (left), Allison (right)

Father and Son

Granddaughter Scout

Granddaughter Amelie

Granddaughter Jocelyn

Grandson Lucas

Grandson Jackson

Granddaughter Lily

Granddaughter Ellie, with Grandpa in the background

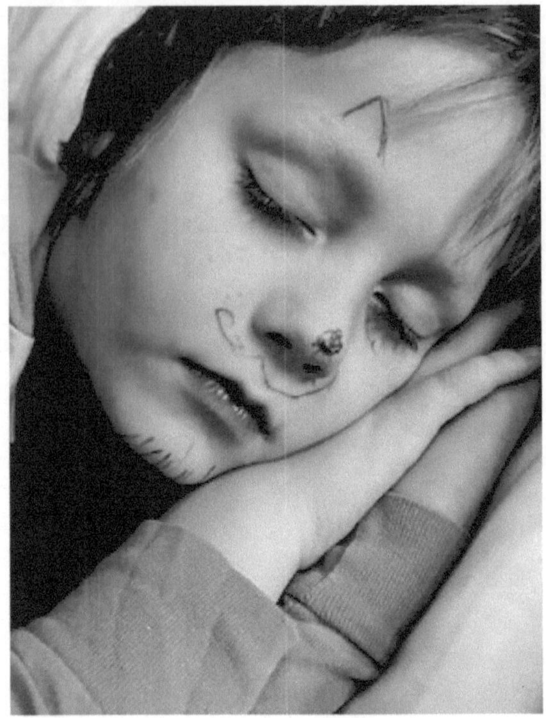

Grandson Owen. It's always Halloween when Owen is around

POSTSCRIPT

Throughout these *AH HA!* moments, the essential starting point was always to identify the purpose, then set out to do everything possible to achieve that purpose. *Everything!*

Here are some examples from my life, and in the pages of this book.

- Reduce violent crime in all categories: murder, rape, armed robbery, and aggravated assault
- Bring business back to downtown Dallas
- Get elected to Congress in 1982 with a total of eleven opponents and two different Districts
- Pass good legislation and defeat bad legislation
- Pass into law civil rights for persons with disabilities
- Create a trade association of one hundred of the largest financial institutions
- Marry Gail and raise three excellent children to adulthood

All these purposes seemed virtually unachievable at the beginning, even marrying Gail (remember her very first words to me). Yet all were achieved.

The power of purpose is, well, powerful. The first step is both the hardest and the easiest: *identify your purpose.*

Then, *write it down*, tattoo it on your forehead if you must. (Recall "Get There Early and Stay Late" when I arrived in Congress)

Then, *focus all your energy* on achieving that purpose. Do whatever it takes (remember Little Red in Chapter One).

You may not achieve it exactly as you first envisioned, but you will achieve something related.

I thank you for reading these *AH HA!* moments and reflections on the power of purpose. I would be delighted to hear your comments, reactions, criticisms, or questions.

As I used to say in starting Town Halls: *"Ask a question and watch me fumble around for the answer, or give me the answer and I will ponder about the question."*

Feel free to email me at **stevebartlettpurpose@gmail.com** with a question, an answer, or, if you dare, share your purpose.

AH HA! **Find your purpose**

I appreciate your interest in my book and value your feedback. I would appreciate it if you could leave your invaluable review on Amazon.com with your feedback, so everyone can read your reactions. Thank you!

About the Author

Steve Bartlett, former U.S. Congressman, Mayor of Dallas, and Financial Services Trade Association CEO. His family and faith have always been paramount. From his early days on the farm to his work with Young Republicans, from business to politics to mentoring young people, he has lived a life with purpose.

INDEX

Since this book is quite informal, I often used first names, sometimes without the last name added at all. Therefore, this index will be alphabetical by first name, with last name added if appropriate.

www.ingramcontent.com/pod-product-compliance
Lightning Source LLC
LaVergne TN
LVHW041103080826
845145LV00007B/1672